D1624396

Samuel R. Wells's

HOW TO BEHAVE

Samuel R. Wells's

HOW TO BEHAVE

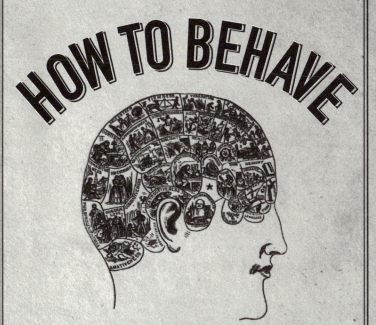

THE CLASSIC POCKET MANUAL OF
Good Manners

Model Behavior

SAMUEL R. WELLS

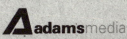

Aadams media

Avon, Massachusetts

Original text from *How To Behave: A Pocket Manual Of Republican Etiquette, And Guide To Correct Personal Habits* by Samuel R. Wells; originally published in 1857 by Fowler & Wells Co., Publishers, 753 Broadway, New York, NY. The text has been edited by F+W Media, Inc., for the modern reader and also to conform with current grammatical standards.

Published by
Adams Media, a division of F+W Media, Inc.
57 Littlefield Street, Avon, MA 02322. U.S.A.
www.adamsmedia.com

ISBN 10: 1-4405-5634-2
ISBN 13: 978-1-4405-5634-0
eISBN 10: 1-4405-5635-0
eISBN 13: 978-1-4405-5635-7

Printed in the United States of America.

10   9   8   7   6   5   4   3   2   1

Library of Congress Cataloging-in-Publication Data

Wells, Samuel R. (Samuel Roberts), 1820–1875.
[How to behave]
Samuel R. Wells's How to behave / Samuel R. Wells.
p. cm.
Originally published: How to behave. New York : Fowler and Wells, 1857, in series: Hand-books for home improvement ; 3.
Includes bibliographical references and index.
ISBN 978-1-4405-5634-0 (paper over board) – ISBN 1-4405-5634-2 (paper over board) – ISBN 978-1-4405-5635-7 (ebook) – ISBN 1-4405-5635-0 (ebook)
1. Etiquette–United States. I. Title.
BJ1853.W46 2012
395–dc23
2012030074

Interior illustrations © iStockPhoto.com/asimetric, 123rf.com.

This book is available at quantity discounts for bulk purchases.
For information, please call 1-800-289-0963.

CONTENTS

INTRODUCTION TO THIS EDITION

The author of this etiquette and manual, Samuel Roberts Wells (1820–1875), was a renowned phrenologist, lecturer, and writer. He was one of the first strong proponents of vegetarianism —which is not difficult to guess based on his suggestions in Chapter I ("If you eat meat, partake sparingly of it"). When Wells wrote this book in 1857, the United States was entering a time of great turmoil. Industrialization had led to significant changes in the national economy, farming, and manufacturing. Waves of European immigrants arrived, leading to lifestyle clashes among different ethnicities. Issues of slavery abounded—the Civil War would begin only a few years later.

Despite the tumultuous cultural landscape, Wells felt the people of the United States should act properly in every aspect of their lives. Thus, his primer touches on nearly every facet of etiquette—dining, dress, conversation, relationships, special occasions, politics—that his readers would have encountered.

Amazingly, even more than 150 years later, most of his advice is still immediately relevant. Sure, at times, you need to remember Wells's historical context—he allows ladies to skip the sections on drinking alcohol and smoking (since he assumes they do neither), and outlines proper behavior when riding in a stagecoach. Regardless, his advice can easily be applied to modern behaviors and modes of transportation. After all, wouldn't you like to remind that annoying cell phone user on the subway to avoid "indulg[ing] in loud talking, in boisterous and untimely laughter, or in profane or vulgar language" . . . or tell your talkative coworker that "all interruptions . . . are not only out of order, but rude in the extreme"? And, isn't it always sound advice to "go out of your way, if necessary, to perform acts of kindness and friendship"?

Wells's timeless guidance is a great reminder for all of us to hearken back to a simpler time when visitors left calling cards instead of voicemails, clothes were modest and properly tailored, and dinner parties involved organized dances . . .

PREFACE

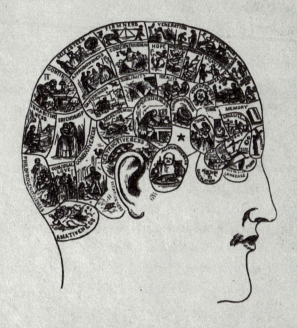

This is an honest and earnest little book, if it has no other merit; and has been prepared expressly for the use of the young people of the United States whom it is designed to aid in becoming, what we are convinced they all desire to be, true American ladies and gentlemen.

Desiring to make our readers something better than mere imitators of foreign manners, often based on social conditions radically different from our own—something better than imitators of *any* manners, in fact—we have dwelt at greater length and with far more emphasis upon general principles than upon special observances, though the latter have their place in our work. It has been our first object to impress upon their minds the fact that good manners and good morals rest upon the same basis, and that justice and benevolence can no more be satisfied without the one than without the other.

[W]e have aimed at usefulness rather than originality; but our plan being radically different from that of most other manuals of etiquette, we have been able to avail ourselves to only a very limited extent of the labors of others, except in the matter of mere conventional forms.

Sensible of the imperfections of our work, but hoping that it will do some acceptable service in the cause of good manners, and aid, in a humble way, in the building up of a truly American and republican school of politeness, we now submit it, with great deference, to a discerning public.

INTRODUCTION

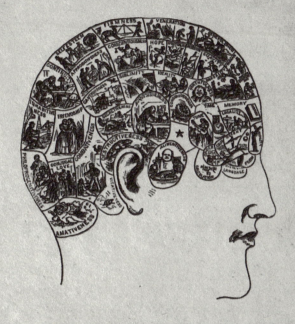

Someone has defined politeness as "only an elegant form of justice"; but it is something more. It is the result of the combined action of all the moral and social feelings, guided by judgment and refined by taste. It requires the exercise of benevolence, veneration (in its human aspect), adhesiveness, and ideality, as well as of conscientiousness. It is the spontaneous recognition of human solidarity—the flowering of philanthropy—the fine art of the social passions. It is to the heart what music is to the ear, and painting and sculpture to the eye. . . .

Politeness itself is always the same. The rules of etiquette, which are merely the forms in which it finds expression, vary with time and place. A sincere regard for the rights of others, in the smallest matters as well as the largest, genuine kindness of heart; good taste, and self-command, which are the foundations of good manners, are never out of fashion; and a person who possesses them can hardly be rude or discourteous, however far he may transgress conventional usages: lacking these qualities, the most perfect knowledge of the rules of etiquette and the strictest observance of them will not suffice to make one truly polite.

"Politeness," says Jean de La Bruyère, a French moralist, "seems to be a certain care, by the manner of our words and actions, to make others pleased with us and themselves." This definition refers the matter directly to those qualities of mind and heart already enumerated as the foundations of good manners. To the same effect is the remark of French writer Madame Élisabeth Celnart, that "the grand secret of never-failing propriety of deportment is *to have an intention of always doing right*."

Some persons have the "instinct of courtesy" so largely developed that they seem hardly to need culture at all. They are equal to any occasion, however novel. They never commit blunders, or if they do commit them, they seem not to be blunders at all. So there are those who sing, speak, or draw intuitively—by inspiration. The great majority of us, however, must be content to acquire these arts by study and practice. In the same way we must acquire the art of behavior, so far as behavior is an art. We must possess, in the first place, a sense of equity, goodwill toward our fellow men, kind feelings, magnanimity, and self-control. Cultivation will do the rest. But we must never forget that manners as well as morals are founded on certain eternal principles, and that while "the *letter* killeth," "the *spirit* giveth *life*."

The account which Lord Chesterfield gives of the method by which he acquired the reputation of being the most polished man in England is a strong example of the efficacy of practice, in view of which no one need despair. He was naturally singularly deficient in that grace which afterward so distinguished him. "I had a strong desire," he says, "to please, and was sensible that I had nothing but the desire. I therefore resolved, if possible, to acquire the means too. I studied attentively and minutely the dress, the air, the manner, the address, and the turn of conversation of all those whom I found to be the people in fashion, and most generally allowed to please. I imitated them as well as I could: if I heard that one man was reckoned remarkably genteel, I carefully watched his dress, motions, and attitudes, and formed my own upon them. When I heard of another whose conversation was agreeable and engaging I listened and attended to the turn of it. I addressed myself, though *de très mauvaise grâce* [with a very bad grace], to all the most fashionable fine ladies; confessed and laughed with them at my own awkwardness and rawness, recommending myself as an object for them to try their skill in forming."

Lord Francis Bacon, English philosopher, says: "To attain good manners it almost sufficeth not to despise them, and that if a man labor too much to express them, he shall lose their grace, which is to be natural and unaffected."

To these testimonies we may add the observation of French author François La Rochefoucauld, that "in manners there are no good copies, for besides that the copy is almost always clumsy or exaggerated, the air which is suited to one person sits ill upon another."

The greater must have been the genius of Lord Chesterfield that enabled him to make the graces of others his own, appropriating them only so far as they *fitted him*, instead of blindly and servilely imitating his models. . . .

Believing that the natural qualities essential to the character of the gentleman or the lady exist in a high degree among our countrymen and countrywomen, and that they universally desire to develop these qualities, and to add to them the necessary knowledge of all the truly significant and living forms and usages of good society, we have written the work now before you. We have not the vanity to believe that the mere reading of it will, of itself, convert an essentially vulgar person into a lady or a gentleman; but we do hope that we have furnished those who most need it with available and efficient aid; and in this hope we dedicate this little "Manual of Republican Etiquette" to all who are, or would be, in the highest sense of these terms,

TRUE REPUBLICAN LADIES OR GENTLEMEN.

Chapter I

PERSONAL HABITS

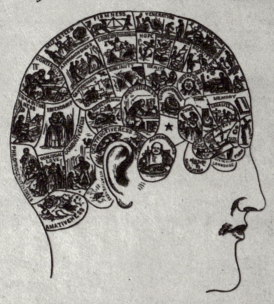

Attention to the person
is the first necessity of good manners.

—Anonymous

WHERE TO COMMENCE

If you wish to commence aright the study of manners, you must make your own person the first lesson. If you neglect this, you will apply yourself to those which follow with very little profit. Omit, therefore, any other chapter in the book rather than this.

The proper care and adornment of the person is a social as well as an individual duty. You have a right to go about with unwashed hands and face, and to wear soiled and untidy garments, perhaps, but you have no right to offend the senses of others by displaying such hands, face, and garments in society. Other people have rights as well as yourself, and no right of yours can extend so far as to infringe theirs.

But we may safely assume that no reader of these pages wishes to render himself disgusting or even disagreeable or to cut himself off from the society of his fellow-men. We address those who seek social intercourse and desire to please. *They* will not think our words amiss, even though they may seem rather "personal," since we have their highest good in view, and speak in the most friendly spirit. Those who do not need our hints and suggestions under this head, and to whom none of our remarks may apply, will certainly have the courtesy to excuse them for the sake of those to whom they will be useful.

CLEANLINESS

"Cleanliness is akin to godliness," it is said. It is not less closely related to gentility. First of all, then, keep yourself scrupulously clean—not your hands and face merely, but your whole person, from the crown of your head to the sole of your foot. Silk stockings may hide dirty feet and ankles from the eye, but they often reveal themselves to another sense, when the possessor little dreams of such an exposure. It is far better to dress coarsely and out of fashion and be strictly clean than to cover a dirty skin with the finest and richest clothing. A coarse shirt or a calico dress is not necessarily vulgar, but dirt is essentially so. We do not here refer, of course, to one's condition while engaged in his or her industrial occupation. Soiled hands and even a begrimed face are badges of honor in the field, the workshop, or the kitchen, but in a country in which soap and water abound, there is no excuse for carrying them into the parlor or the dining room.

> It is far better to dress coarsely and out of fashion and be strictly clean than to cover a dirty skin with the finest and richest clothing.

A clean skin is as essential to health, beauty, and personal comfort as it is to decency; and without health and that perfect freedom from physical disquiet which comes only from the normal action of all the functions of the bodily organs, your behavior can never be satisfactory to yourself or agreeable to others. Let us urge you, then, to give this matter your first attention.

The Daily Bath

To keep clean, you must bathe frequently. In the first place you should wash the whole body with pure soft water every morning on rising from your bed, rubbing it till dry with a coarse towel, and afterward using friction with the hands. If you have not been at all accustomed to cold bathing, commence with tepid water, lowering the temperature by degrees till that which is perfectly cold becomes agreeable. In warm weather, comfort and cleanliness alike require still more frequent bathing.

Mohammed made frequent ablutions a religious duty; and in that he was right. The rank and fetid odors that exhale from a foul skin can hardly be neutralized by the sweetest incense of devotion.

Soap and Water

But the daily bath of which we have spoken is not suffi-cient. In addition to the pores from which exudes the watery fluid called perspiration, the skin is furnished with innu-merable minute openings, known as the sebaceous follicles, which pour over its surface a thin limpid oil anointing it and rendering it soft and supple; but also causing the dust as well as the effete matter thrown out by the pores to adhere, and, if allowed to accumulate, finally obstructing its functions and causing disease. It also, especially in warm weather, emits an exceedingly disagreeable odor. Pure cold water will not wholly remove these oily accumulations. The occasional use of soap and warm or tepid water is therefore necessary; but all washings with soapy or warm water should be followed by a thorough rinsing with pure cold water.

Use good, fine soap. The common coarser kinds are generally too strongly alkaline and have an unpleasant effect upon the skin.

The Feet

The feet are particularly liable to become offensively odor-iferous, especially when the perspiration is profuse. Frequent washings with cold water, with the occasional use of warm water and soap, are absolutely necessary to cleanliness.

Change of Clothes

A frequent change of linen is another essential of cleanli-ness. It avails little to wash the body if we enclose it the next minute in soiled garments. It is not in the power of everyone to wear fine and elegant clothes, but we can all, under ordinary circumstances, afford clean shirts, drawers, and stockings. Never sleep in any garment worn during the day; and your nightdress should be well aired every morning.

The Nails

You will not, of course, go into company, or sit down to the table, with soiled hands, but unless you habituate your-self to a special care of them, more or less dirt will be found lodged under the nails. Clean them carefully every time you wash your hands, and keep them smoothly and evenly cut. If you allow them to get too long they are liable to be broken off, and become uneven and ragged, and if you pare them too closely they fail to protect the ends of the fingers.

The Head

The head is more neglected, perhaps, than any other part of the body. The results are not less disastrous here than elsewhere. Dandruff forms, dust accumulates, the scalp becomes diseased, the hair grows dry and falls off, and, if the evil be not remedied, premature baldness ensues.

The head should be thoroughly washed as often as cleanliness demands. This will not injure the hair, as many suppose, but, on the contrary, will promote its growth and add to its beauty. If soap is used, however, it should be carefully rinsed off. If the hair is carefully and *thoroughly* brushed every morning, it will not require very frequent washings. If the scalp be kept in a healthy condition the hair will be moist, glossy, and luxuriant, and no oil or hair wash will be required; and these preparations generally do more harm than good.

> **Washing your hair will promote its growth and add to its beauty.**

Nightcaps are most unwholesome and uncleanly contrivances, and should be discarded altogether. They keep the head unnaturally warm, shut out the fresh air, and shut in those natural exhalations which should be allowed to pass off, and thus weaken the hair and render it more liable to fall off. Ladies may keep their hair properly together during repose by wearing a *net* over it.

The Teeth

Do not forget the teeth. Cleanliness, health, a pure breath, and the integrity and durability of those organs require that they be thoroughly and effectually scoured with the tooth-brush dipped in soft water, with the addition of a little soap, if necessary, every morning. Brush them outside and inside, and in every possible direction. You cannot be too careful in this matter. After brushing, rinse your mouth with cold water. A slighter brushing should be given them after each meal. Use an ivory toothpick or a quill to remove any particles of food that may be lodged between the teeth.

> Use an ivory toothpick or a quill to remove any particles of food that may be lodged between the teeth.

There are, no doubt, original differences in teeth, as in other parts of the human system, some being more liable to decay than others; but the simple means we have pointed out, if adopted in season and perseveringly applied, will pre-serve almost any teeth, in all their usefulness and reality, till old age. If yours have been neglected, and some of them are already decayed, hasten to preserve the remainder. While you have *any* teeth left, it is never too late to begin to take care of them; and if you have children, do not, we entreat you, neglect *their* teeth. If the first or temporary teeth are cared for and preserved, they will be mainly absorbed by the second or permanent ones, and will drop out of themselves. The others, in that case, will come out regular and even.

Your toothbrushes should be rather soft; those which are too hard injuring both the teeth and the gums.

THE BREATH

A bad breath arises more frequently than otherwise from neglected and decayed teeth. If it is occasioned by a foul stomach, a pure diet, bathing, water injections, and a general attention to the laws of health are required for its removal.

EATING & DRINKING

Whatever has a bearing upon health has at least an indirect connection with manners; the reader will therefore excuse us for introducing here a few remarks that may seem, at the first glance, rather irrelevant. Sound lungs, a healthy liver, and a good digestion are as essential to the right performance of our social duties as they are to our own personal comfort; therefore a few words on eating and drinking, as affecting these, will not be out of place.

WHAT TO EAT

An unperverted appetite is the highest authority in matters of diet. In fact, its decisions should be considered final, and without the privilege of appeal. Nature makes no mistakes.

But appetite, like all the other instincts or feelings of our nature, is liable to become perverted, and to lead us astray. We acquire a relish for substances that are highly hurtful, such as tobacco, ardent spirits, malt liquors, and the like. We have "sought out many inventions," to pander to false and fatal tastes, and too often eat, not to sustain life and promote the harmonious development of the system, but to poison the very fountains of our being and implant in our blood the seeds of disease.

> ## Eating without appetite is one of the most fatal of common errors.

Attend to the demands of appetite, but use all your judgment in determining whether it is a natural, undepraved craving of the system that speaks, or an acquired and vicious taste, and give or withhold accordingly; and, above all, never eat when you have *no appetite*. Want of appetite is equivalent to the most authoritative command to *eat nothing*, and we disregard it at our peril. Food, no matter how wholesome, taken into our stomachs under such circumstances, instead of being digested and appropriated, becomes rank poison. *Eating without appetite is one of the most fatal of common errors. . . .*

Live well. A generous diet promotes vitality and capability for action. "Good cheer is friendly to health." But do not confound a generous diet with what is usually called "rich" food. Let all your dishes be nutritious, but plain, simple, and wholesome. Avoid highly seasoned victuals and very greasy food at all times, but particularly in warm weather, also too much nutriment in the highly condensed forms of sugar, syrup, honey, and the like.

If you eat meat, partake sparingly of it, especially in summer. We Americans are the greatest meat-eaters in the world, and it is not unreasonable to believe that there may be some connection between this fact and the equally notorious one that we are the most unhealthy people in the world. An untold amount of disease results from the too-free use of meat during the hot months. Heat promotes putrefaction; and as this change in meat is very rapid in warm weather, we cannot be too careful not to eat that which is in the slightest degree tainted. Even when it goes into the stomach in a normal condition, there is danger; for if too much is eaten, or the digestive organs are not sufficiently strong and active, the process of putrefaction may commence in the stomach and diffuse a subtle poison through the whole system.

> We Americans are the greatest meat-eaters in the world, and it is not unreasonable to believe that there may be some connection between this fact and the equally notorious one that we are the most unhealthy people in the world.

Hot biscuits; *hot* griddle cakes, saturated with butter and Stuart's syrup; and *hot* coffee, scarcely modified at all by the small quantity of milk usually added, are among the most deleterious articles ever put upon a table. While these continue to be the staples of our breakfasts, healthy stomachs and clear complexions will be rare among us. Never eat or drink *anything* HOT.

Good bread is an unexceptionable article of diet. The best is made of unbolted wheat flour. A mixture of wheat and rye flour, or of cornmeal with either, makes excellent bread. The meal and flour should be freshly ground; they deteriorate by being kept long. If raised or fermented bread is required, hop yeast is the best ferment that can be used.

> **Beans and peas should be more generally eaten than they are. They are exceedingly nutritious, and very palatable.**

Beans and peas should be more generally eaten than they are. They are exceedingly nutritious, and very palatable. In New England, "pork and beans" hold the place of honor, but elsewhere in this country they are almost unknown. Leaving out the pork (which, personally, we hold in more than Jewish abhorrence), nothing can be better, provided they are eaten in moderation and with a proper proportion of less nutritious food. They should be well baked in pure, soft water. A sufficient quantity of salt to season them, with the addition of a little sweet milk, cream, or butter while baking, leaves nothing to be desired. If meat is wanted, however, a slice of beefsteak, laid upon the surface, will serve a better purpose than pork. Potatoes, beets, turnips, carrots, parsnips, and cabbages are good in their place.

Nature indicates very plainly that fruits and berries, in their season, should have a prominent place in our diet. They are produced in abundance, and every healthy stomach instinctively craves them. Strawberries, blackberries, raspberries, whortleberries, cherries, plums, grapes, figs, apples, pears, peaches, and melons are "food fit for gods." We pity those whose perverted taste or digestion leads to their rejection. But some are *afraid* to eat fruits and berries, particularly in midsummer, just the time when nature and common sense say they should be eaten most freely.

Unripe fruits should be scrupulously avoided, and that which is in any measure decayed as scarcely less objectionable. Fruit and berries should make a part of every meal in summer. In winter they are less necessary, but may be eaten with advantage, if within our reach; and they are easily preserved in various ways.

When to Eat

Eat when the stomach, through the instinct of appetite, demands a new supply of food. If all your habits are regular, this will be at about the same hours each day; and regularity in the time of taking our meals is very important. Want of attention to this point is a frequent cause of derangement of the digestive organs. We cannot stop to discuss the question how many meals per day we should eat; but whether you eat one, two, or three, never, under ordinary circumstances, take lunches. The habit of eating between meals is a most pernicious one. Not even your children must be indulged in it, as you value their health, comfort, and good behavior.

How Much to Eat

We cannot tell you, by weight or measure, how much
to eat, the right quantity depending much upon age, sex,
occupation, season, and climate, but the quantity is quite as
important as the quality. Appetite would be a sure guide in
both respects were it not so often perverted and diseased. As
a general rule, we eat too much. It is better to err in the other
direction. An uncomfortable feeling of fullness, or of dullness
and stupor after a meal, is a sure sign of overeating, so whatever and whenever you eat, *eat slowly, masticate your food
well*, and DO NOT EAT TOO MUCH.

> **Whether you eat one, two, or three meals, never, under
> ordinary circumstances, take lunches.**

Drink

If we eat proper food, and in proper quantity, we are
seldom thirsty. Inordinate thirst indicates a feverish state of
either the stomach or the general system. It is pretty sure to
follow a too hearty meal.

Water is the proper drink for everybody and for everything
that lives or grows. It should be pure and soft. Many diseases
arise wholly from the use of unwholesome water. If you drink
tea (which we do not recommend), let it be the best of black
tea, and *not* strong. Coffee, if drunk at all, should be diluted
with twice its quantity of boiled milk, and well sweetened with
white sugar.

BREATHING

Breathing is as necessary as eating. If we cease to breathe, our bodies cease to live. If we only *half* breathe, as is often the case, we only half live. The human system requires a constant supply of oxygen to keep up the vital processes that closely resemble combustion, of which oxygen is the prime supporter. If the supply is insufficient, the fire of life wanes.

> **Breathe good air. Have all your rooms, and especially your sleeping apartment, well ventilated.**

The healthy condition of the lungs also requires that they be completely expanded by the air inhaled. The imperfect breathing of many persons fails to accomplish the required inflation, and the lungs become diseased for want of their natural action. Full, deep breathing and pure air are as essential to health, happiness, and the right performance of our duties, whether individual, political, or social, as pure food and temperate habits of eating and drinking are. Attend, then, to the lungs as well as the stomach. Breathe good air. Have all your rooms, and especially your sleeping apartment, well ventilated. The air that has been spoiled by breathing or by smoke, which abstracts the oxygen and supplies its place with carbonic acid gas, is a *subtle poison*.

EXERCISE

The amount of physical exercise required varies with age, sex, and temperament; but no person can enjoy vigorous health without a considerable degree of active bodily exertion. Four or five hours per day spent in the open air, in some labor or amusement that calls for the exercise of the muscles of the body, is probably no more than a proper average. We can live with less—that is, for a short time; but Nature's laws are inexorable, and we cannot escape the penalty affixed to their violation.

Those whose occupations are sedentary should seek amusements that require the exertion of the physical powers, and should spend as much as possible of their leisure time in the open air. We must, however, use good judgment in this matter as well as in eating. Too much exercise at once, or that which is fitful and violent, is often exceedingly injurious to those whose occupations have accustomed them to little physical exertion of any kind.

The women of our country are suffering incalculably for want of proper exercise. No other single cause perhaps is doing so much to destroy health and beauty, and deteriorate the race, as this. "Your women are very handsome," Swedish writer and feminist Frederika Bremer said, "but they are too white; they look as if they grew in the shade." A sad truth. Ladies, if you would be healthy, beautiful, and attractive—if you would fit yourselves to be good wives, and the mothers of strong and noble men, you *must* take an adequate amount of exercise in the open air. *This should be an everyday duty.*

THE COMPLEXION

Every person, and especially every lady, desires a clear complexion. To secure this, follow the directions in this chapter
in reference to cleanliness, eating, drinking, breathing, and
exercise. The same recipe serves for ruby lips and rosy cheeks.
These come and go with health, and health depends upon obe-
dience to the laws of our constitution.

GENERAL HINTS

Few of us are free from disagreeable habits of which we are
hardly conscious, so seemingly natural have they become to us.
It is the obligation of friendship, though not always a pleasant
one, to point them out. It is our business to assume that obligation here, finding our excuse in the necessity of the case. Our
bad habits not only injure ourselves, but they give offense to
others, and indirectly injure them also.

Tobacco

Ladies, in this country, do not use tobacco, so they may
skip this section. A large and increasing number of gentlemen
may do the same; but if you use tobacco, in any form, allow us
to whisper a useful hint or two in your ear.

Smoking, snuff-taking, and especially chewing, are bad habits at best, and in their coarser forms highly disgusting to pure and refined people, and especially to ladies. You have the same right to smoke, take snuff, and chew that you have to indulge in the luxuries of a filthy skin and soiled garments, but you have no right, in either case, to do violence to the senses and sensibilities of other people by their exhibition in society.

Smoke if you will, chew, take snuff (against our earnest advice, however), make yourself generally and particularly disagreeable, but you must suffer the consequences—the social outlawry—that must result. Shall we convert our parlors into tobacco shops, risk the ruin of our carpets and furniture from the random shots of your disgusting saliva, and fill the whole atmosphere of our house with a pungent stench, to the discomfort and disgust of everybody else, merely for the pleasure of your company? We have rights as well as you, one of which is to exclude from our circle all persons whose manners or habits are distasteful to us. You talk of rights. You cannot blame others for exercising theirs.

> Smoke if you will, chew, take snuff (against our earnest advice, however), make yourself generally and particularly disagreeable, but you must suffer the consequences—social outlawry.

There are degrees here as everywhere else. One may chew a *little*, smoke an *occasional* cigar, and take a pinch of snuff *now* and *then*, and if he never indulges in these habits in the presence of others, and is very careful to purify his person before going into company, he may confine the bad effects, which he cannot escape, *mostly* to his own person. But he must not smoke in any parlor, or sitting-room, or dining-room, or sleeping chamber, or in the street, and particularly not in the presence of ladies, *anywhere*.

Spitting

"The use of tobacco has made us a nation of spitters," as someone has truly remarked. Spitting is a private act, and tobacco users are not alone in violating good taste and good manners by hawking and spitting in company. You should never be seen to spit. Use your handkerchief carefully and so as not to be noticed, or, in case of necessity, leave the room.

Gin and Gentility

The spirit and tenor of our remarks on tobacco will apply to the use of ardent spirits. The fumes of gin, whisky, and rum are, if possible, worse than the scent of tobacco. They must on no account be brought into company. If a man (this is another section that women may skip) will make a beast of himself, and fill his blood with liquid poison, he must, if he desires admission into good company, do it either privately or with companions whose senses and appetites are as depraved as his own.

Onions, Etc.

All foods or drinks that taint the breath or cause disagreeable gas should be avoided by persons going into company. Onions emit so very disagreeable an odor that no truly polite person will eat them when liable to inflict their fumes upon others. Particular care should be taken to guard against a bad breath from *any* cause.

SEVERAL ITEMS

Never do any of the following in the presence of others:

- pare or scrape your nails
- pick your teeth
- comb your hair, or
- perform any of the necessary operations of the toilet.

All these things should be carefully attended to in the privacy of your own room. To pick the nose, dig the ears, or scratch the head or any part of the person in company is still worse. Watch yourself carefully, and if you have any such habits, break them up at once. These may seem little things, but they have their weight, and go far in determining the character of the impression we make upon those around us.

Chapter II

DRESS

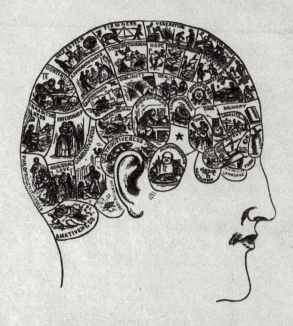

From little matters let us pass to less,
And lightly touch the mysteries of dress;
The outward forms the inner man reveal;
We guess the pulp before we eat the peel.

—O. W. Holmes

THE LANGUAGE OF DRESS

Dress has its language, which is, or may be, read and understood by all. It is one of the forms in which we naturally give expression to our tastes, our constructive faculties, our reason, our feelings, our habits—in a word, to our character, as a whole. This expression is often greatly modified by the arbitrary laws of Fashion, and by circumstances of time, place, and condition, which we cannot wholly control; but can hardly be entirely falsified. Even that arch tyrant, the reigning *Mode*, whatever it may be, leaves us little room for choice in materials, forms, and colors, and the choice we make indicates our prominent traits of character.

THE USES OF DRESS

"Dress," that admirable art journal *The Crayon* says, "has two functions—to clothe and to ornament; and while we cannot lose sight of either point, we must not attribute to the one a power which belongs to the other. The essential requirement of dress is to cover and make comfortable the body, and of two forms of dress that fulfill this function equally well, that is the better which is most accordant with the laws of beauty. . . . Fit is the primary demand; and *the dress that appears uncomfortable is untasteful.*

"But in the secondary function of dress, ornamentation, there are several diverse objects to be attained—dignity, grace, vivacity, brilliancy—qualities distinguishing different individuals, and indicating the impression they wish to make on society, and are expressed by different combinations of the elements of beauty, line, or form, and color. When the appareling of the outer being is in most complete harmony with the mental constitution, the taste is fullest."

THE ART OF DRESS

True art adapts dress to its uses, as indicated in the previous extract. It is based on universal principles fundamental to all art.

The art-writer already quoted says, very truly, that "dress is always to be considered as secondary to the person." This is a fundamental maxim in the art of costume, but is often lost sight of, and dress made *obtrusive* at the expense of the individuality of the wearer. A man's vest or cravat must not seem a too important part of him. Dress may heighten beauty, but it cannot create it. If you are not better and more beautiful than your clothes, you are, indeed, a man or a woman of straw.

The next principle to be regarded is the *fit* of your costume, in its forms, materials, and colors, to your person and circumstances, and to the conditions of the time, place, and occasion on which it is to be worn. Fashion often compels us to violate this principle, and dress in the most absurd, incongruous, unbecoming, and uncomfortable style. A little more self-respect and independence, however, would enable us to resist many of her most preposterous enactments. But Fashion is not responsible for all the incongruities in dress with which we meet. They are often the result of bad taste and affectation.

The first demand of this law of "fit"ness is, that your costume shall accord with your person. The young and the old, we all instinctively know, should not dress alike. Neither should the tall and the short, the dark and the light, the pale and the rosy, the grave and the gay, the tranquil and the vivacious. Each variety of form, color, and character has its appropriate style; but our space here is too limited to allow us to do more than drop a hint toward what each requires, to produce the most harmonious and effective combination.

According to *Hints Toward Physical Perfection; or, How to Acquire and Retain Beauty, Grace, and Strength, and Secure Long Life and Perpetual Youth*, "In form, simplicity and long, unbroken lines give dignity, while complicated and short lines express vivacity. Curves, particularly if long and sweeping, give grace while straight lines and angles indicate power and strength. In color, unity of tint gives repose—if somber, gravity but if light and clear, then a joyous serenity—variety of tint giving vivacity, and if contrasted, brilliancy." Further advice:

- Longitudinal stripes in a lady's dress make her appear taller than she really is, and are therefore appropriate for persons of short stature. Tall women, for this reason, should never wear them.
- Flounces are becoming to tall persons, but not to short ones.
- The colors worn should be determined by the complexion, and should harmonize with it. "Ladies with delicate rosy complexions bear white and blue better than dark colors, while sallow hues of complexion will not bear these colors near them, and require dark, quiet, or grave colors to improve their appearance. Yellow is the most trying and dangerous of all, and can only be worn by the rich-toned, healthy-looking brunette."

There should be harmony between your dress and your circumstances. It should accord with your means, your house, your furniture, the place in which you reside, and the society in which you move.

> The young and the old, we all instinctively know, should not dress alike.

Your costume should be suited to the time, place, and occasion on which it is to be worn. That summer clothes should not be worn in winter, or winter clothes in summer, everyone sees clearly enough. [Y]ou should have one dress for the kitchen, the field, or the workshop, and another, and quite a different one, for the parlor; one for the street and another for the carriage, one for a ride on horseback and another for a ramble in the country. Long, flowing, and even trailing skirts are beautiful and appropriate in the parlor, but in the muddy streets, draggling in the filth, and embarrassing every movement of the wearer, or in the country among the bushes and briers, they lose all their beauty and grace, because no longer fitting.

> Rational independence, good taste, and the study of art are preparing the way for the complete overthrow of arbitrary fashion.

The prettiest costume we have ever seen for a shopping excursion or a walk in the city, and especially for a ramble in the country, is:

- A short dress or frock reaching to the knee.
- Trousers of the common pantaloon form, but somewhat wider. (Full Turkish trousers might be worn with this dress, but are less convenient.)
- The waist or body of the dress is made with a yoke and belt, and pretty full.
- The sleeves should be gathered into a band and buttoned at the wrist.

- A sash . . . of a different color from the waist has a fine effect as a part of this costume.
- Add to it a wide-brimmed hat and good substantial shoes or boots, and you may walk with ease, grace, and pleasure. If you reside in a place where you can adopt this as your industrial and walking costume, without too much notoriety and odium, try it. You must judge of this for yourself. We are telling you what is fitting, comfortable, and healthful, and therefore, in its place, beautiful, and not what it is expedient for you to wear. The time is coming when such a costume may be worn anywhere. Rational independence, good taste, and the study of art are preparing the way for the complete overthrow of arbitrary fashion. Help us to hasten the time when both women and men shall be permitted to dress as the eternal principles, harmony and beauty, dictate, and be no longer the slaves of the tailor and the dressmaker.

But without adopting any innovations liable to shock staid conservatism or puritanic prudery, you may still, in a good measure, avoid the incongruities which we are now compelled to witness, and make your costume accord with place and occupation:

Gentlemen
- In the field, garden, and workshop, gentlemen can wear nothing more comfortable and graceful than the blouse. It may be worn loose or confined by a belt.
- If your occupation is a very dusty one, wear overalls.

- In the counting-room and office, gentlemen wear [more fitted] frock-coats or [looser] sack coats. They need not be of very fine material, and should not be of any garish pattern.
- In your study or library, and about the house generally, on ordinary occasions, a handsome dressing-gown is comfortable and elegant.

Ladies

- A lady, while performing the morning duties of her household, may wear a plain loose dress, made high in the neck, and with long sleeves fastened at the wrist. It must not look slatternly, and may be exceedingly beautiful and becoming.

MATERIALS, ETC.

The materials of which your clothes are made should be the best that your means will allow. One generally exercises a very bad economy and worse taste in wearing low-priced and coarse materials. For your working costume, the materials should of course correspond with the usage to which they are to be subjected. They should be strong and durable, but need not therefore be either very coarse or at all ugly. As a general rule, it costs no more to dress well than ill.

Shirts

A gentleman's shirts should always be fine, clean, and well-fitted. It is better to wear a coarse or threadbare coat than a disreputable shirt. The better taste and finer instincts of the ladies will require no hint in reference to their "most intimate appareling." True taste, delicacy, and refinement regards the underclothing as scrupulously as that which is exposed to view.

Shoes

The coverings of the head and the feet are important and should by no means be inferior to the rest of your apparel. Shoes are better than boots, except in cases where the latter are required for the protection of the feet and ankles against water, snow, or injury from briers, brambles, and the like. Ladies' shoes for walking should be substantial enough to keep the feet dry and warm. If neatly made, and well-fitting, they need not be clumsy. Thin shoes, worn on the damp ground or pavement, have carried many a beautiful woman to her grave. If you wish to have corns and unshapely feet, wear tight shoes; they never fail to produce those results.

Hats

The fashionable fur hat, in its innumerable but always ugly forms, is, in the eye of taste, an absurd and unsightly covering for the head; and it is hardly less uncomfortable and unhealthful than ugly. The fine, soft, and more picturesque felt hats now, we are glad to say, coming more and more into vogue, are far more comfortable and healthful. A light, fine straw hat is the best for summer.

The bonnets of the ladies, in their fashionable forms, are only a little less ugly and unbecoming than the fur hats of the gentlemen. A broad-brimmed hat is far more becoming to most women than the common bonnet. We hope to live to see both "stove-pipe hats" and "sugar-scoop bonnets" abolished; but, in the meantime, let those wear them who *must*.

> The fashionable fur hat . . . is, in the eye of taste, an absurd and unsightly covering for the head.

MRS. MANNERS ON DRESS

Mrs. Manners, the highest authority we can possibly quote in such matters, has the following hints to girls, which we cannot deny ourselves the pleasure of copying, though they may seem, in part, a repetition of remarks already made:

> "Good taste is indispensable in dress, but that,
> united to neatness, is *all* that is *necessary*—that
> is the fabled cestus of Venus which gave beauty
> to its wearer. Good taste involves *suitable*

fabrics—a neat and becoming 'fitting' to her figure—colors suited to her complexion, and a simple and unaffected manner of wearing one's clothes. A worsted dress in a warm day, or a white one in a cold day, or a light, thin one in a windy day, are all in *bad* taste. Very fine or very delicate dresses worn in the street, or very highly ornamented clothes worn to church or to shop in, are in *bad* taste. Very long dresses worn in muddy or dusty weather, even if long dresses are the *fashion*, are still in *bad* taste.

"Deep and bright-colored gloves are always in bad taste; very few persons are careful enough in selecting gloves. Light shoes and dark dresses, white stockings and dark dresses, dark stockings and light dresses, are not indicative of good taste. A girl with neatly and properly dressed feet, with neat, well-fitting gloves, smoothly arranged hair, and a clean, well-made dress, who walks well, and speaks well, and, above all, acts politely and kindly, *is a lady*, and no *wealth* is required here. Fine clothes and fine airs are abashed before such propriety and good taste. Thus the poorest may be so attired as to appear as lady-like as the wealthiest; nothing is more *vulgar* than the idea that money makes a lady, or that fine clothes can do it."

WEARING THE HAIR & BEARD

The hair and beard, in one of their aspects, belong to the dress. In reference to the style of wearing them, consult the general principles of taste. A man to whom nature has given a handsome beard deforms himself sadly by shaving—at least, that is our opinion; and on this point fashion and good taste agree. The full beard is now more common than the shaven face in all our large cities.

> **A man to whom nature has given a handsome beard deforms himself sadly by shaving.**

In the dressing of the hair there is room for the display of a great deal of taste and judgment. The style should vary with the different forms of face. Lardner's *Young Ladies' Manual* has the following hints to the gentler sex. Gentlemen can modify them to suit their case:

> "After a few experiments, a lady may very easily decide what mode of dressing her hair, and what head-dress renders her face most attractive.

> "Ringlets hanging about the forehead suit almost every one. On the other hand, the fashion of putting the hair smoothly, and drawing

were turning into a universal inquiry as to the sense or propriety of *any fashion at all.* When the subject shall have been fully discussed, and public attention fully awakened, common sense will probably take the direction of the matter, and opinion will settle in some shape which, at least, may reject former excesses and absurdities. Some moderate similarity of dress is doubtless necessary, and there are proper times and places for long dresses and short dresses.

> We venture to express a hope that they will *get rid of the present slavish uniformity*—that what is becoming to each may be worn without fear of unfashionableness.

"These and other points the ladies are likely to come to new decisions about. While they consult health, cleanliness, and convenience, however, we venture to express a hope that they will *get rid of the present slavish uniformity*—that what is becoming to each may be worn without fear of unfashionableness, and that in this way we may see every woman dressed somewhat differently and to her own best advantage, and the *proportion of beauty largely increased*, as it would, thereby, most assuredly be."

Chapter III

SELF-CULTURE

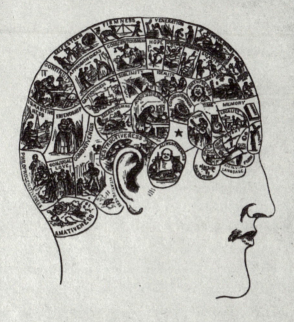

There is no man who can so easily and so naturally become in all points a Gentleman Knight, without fear and without reproach, as a true American Republican.

—James Parton

MORAL & SOCIAL TRAINING

Having given due attention to your personal habits and dress, consider what special errors still remain to be corrected, or what deficiencies to be supplied, and carefully and persever-ingly apply yourself to the required self-training.

If you are sensible of an inadequate development of any of those faculties or feelings on which good manners are based, set yourself at once about the work of cultivation, remembering that the legitimate exercise of any organ or function necessarily tends to its development.

Look first to conscientiousness. It is hardly possible for you to acquire genuine good manners without an acute sense of equity. Accustom yourself to a sacred regard for the rights of others, even in the minutest matters, and in the most familiar intercourse of the family or social circle. In a simi-lar manner cultivate benevolence, veneration, adhesiveness, agreeableness, ideality, and the moral, social, and esthetic faculties in general.

Go out of your way, if necessary, to perform acts of kind-ness and friendship; never omit the "thank you" that is due for the slightest possible favor, whether rendered by the highest or the lowest; be always bland and genial; respect times, places, observances, and especially persons; and put yourself in the way of all possible elevating and refining influences. Manners have their origin in the mind and the heart. Manners do not make the man, as is sometimes asserted; but the man makes the manners. It is true, however, that the manners react upon mind and heart, continually developing and improving the qualities out of which they spring.

> Go out of your way, if necessary, to perform acts of kindness and friendship.

You are placed in a particular community, or you are invited or wish to gain admittance into a certain circle. Different communities and circles require, to some extent, different qualifications. Ascertain what you lack and acquire it as speedily as possible; but remember that good sense and good nature are out of place in no company.

LANGUAGE

Conversation plays an important part in the intercourse of society. It is a great and valuable accomplishment to be able to talk well. Cultivate language and the voice. Learn to express yourself with correctness, ease, and elegance. This subject is worthy of all the time and study you can give to it.

POSITION & MOVEMENT

Study also the graces of manner, motion, and position. Grace is natural, no doubt, but most of us have nearly lost sight of nature. It is often with the greatest difficulty that we find our way back to her paths. It seems a simple and easy thing to walk, and a still easier and simpler thing to stand or sit, but not one in twenty performs either of these acts with ease and grace. There are a hundred little things connected with attitude, movement, the carriage of the arms, the position of the feet, and the like, which, though seemingly unimportant are really essential to elegance and ease. Never despise these little things, or be ashamed to acquire the smallest grace by study and practice.

STANDING

You desire to be a person of "good standing" in society. How *do* you stand? We refer now to the artistic or esthetic point of view. If you are awkward, you are more likely to manifest your awkwardness in standing than in walking. Do you know where to put your feet and what to do with your hands?

In the absence of any better rule or example, try to forget your limbs, and let them take care of themselves. But observe the attitudes which sculptors give to their statues; and study also those of children, which are almost always graceful, because natural. Avoid, on the one hand, the stiffness of the soldier, and, on the other, the ape-like suppleness of the dancing-master; and let there be no straining, no fidgeting, no uneasy shifting of position. You should stand on *both* feet, bearing a little more heavily on one than the other.

> **Let there be no straining, no fidgeting, no uneasy shifting of position.**

SITTING

The same general principles apply to the sitting posture. This may be either graceful, dignified, and elegant, or awkward, abject, and uncouth. The latter class of qualities may be got rid of and the former acquired, and depend upon it, it is a matter of some consequence which of them characterizes your position and movements.

WALKING

Walking is not so difficult an accomplishment as standing and sitting, but should receive due attention. It has a very close connection with character, and either of them may be improved or deteriorated through the other. Mrs. Manners, a close observer and a sensible and trustworthy monitor of her own sex, thus enumerates some of the common faults of women in their "carriage," or manner of walking:

> "Slovenliness in walking characterizes some.
> They go shuffling along, precisely as if their
> shoes were down at the heel—'slipshod'—and
> they could not lift up their feet in consequence.
> If it is dusty or sandy, they kick up the dust
> before them and fill their skirts with it. This

is exceedingly ungraceful. If I were a gentle-man, I really do not think I could marry a lady who walked like this; she would appear so very undignified, and I could not be proud of her.

"Some have another awkwardness. They lift up their feet so high that their knees are sent out before them, showing the movement through the dress. They always seem to be leaving their skirts behind them, instead of carrying them gracefully about them. Some saunter along so loosely they seem to be hung on wires; others are as stiff as if they supposed only straight lines were agreeable to the eye; and others, again, run the chin for-ward considerably in advance of the breast, look-ing very silly and deficient in self-respect.

"Sometimes a lady walks so as to turn up her dress behind every time she puts her foot back, and I have seen a well-dressed woman made to look very awkward by elevating her shoulders slightly and pushing her elbows too far behind her. Some hold their hands up to the waist, and press their arms against themselves as tightly as if they were glued there; others swing them backward and forward, as a businessman walks along the street. *Too-short* steps detract from dignity very much, forming a mincing pace; too-long steps are masculine.

"Some walk upon the ball of the foot very flatly and clumsily; others come down upon the heel as though a young elephant were moving; and others, again, ruin their shoes and their appearance by walking upon the side of the foot. Many practice a stoop called the Grecian bend, and when they are thirty, will pass well, unless the face be seen, for fifty years' old."

SELF-COMMAND

Without perfect self-control you are constantly liable to do something amiss, and your other social qualifications will avail little. You must not only be fully conscious of who you are, what you are, where you are, and what you are about, but you must also have an easy and complete control of all your words and actions, and feel *at home* wherever you are. You are liable to lose this self-command either through bashfulness or excitement.

[Bashfulness] is one of the greatest obstacles with which a majority of young people have to contend. It can be overcome by *resolute effort* and the cultivation of self-respect and self-reliance. Do not allow it to keep you out of society. You will not conquer it by such a course. You might as reasonably expect to learn to swim without going into the water.

OBSERVATION

One of the best means of improvement in manners is observation. In company, where you are in doubt in reference to any rule or form, be quiet and observe what others do, and govern your conduct by theirs; but except in mere external forms, beware of a servile imitation. Seek to understand the principles that underlie the observances you witness, and to become imbued with the spirit of the society (if good) in which you move, rather than to copy particulars in the manners of any one.

PRACTICAL LESSONS

But the most important instrumentality for the promotion of the externals of good manners is constant practice in the actual everyday intercourse of society; and without this our instructions and your study will both be thrown away. Begin now, today, with the next person you meet or address.

Chapter IV

MANNERS AND MORALS

*Courtesy is the beautiful part of morality, justice carried
to the utmost, rectitude refined, magnanimity in trifles.*

—LIFE ILLUSTRATED

RIGHTS

In this country, we need no incitements to the assertion and maintenance of our rights, whether individual or national. We are ready at all times to do battle for them either with the tongue, the pen, or the sword, as the case may require. Even women have discovered that *they* have rights, and he must be a bold man indeed who dares call them into question. Yes, we all, men, women, and children, have rights, and are forward enough in claiming them. Are we equally ready to respect the rights of others?

> Even women have discovered that
> *they* have rights, and he must be a bold man indeed
> who dares call them into question.

DUTIES

Out of rights grow duties; the first of which is to live an honest, truthful, self-loyal life, acting and speaking always and everywhere in accordance with the laws of our being, as revealed in our own physical and mental organization. It is by the light of this fact that we must look upon all social requirements, whether in dress, manners, or morals. All that is fundamental and genuine in these will be found to harmonize with universal principles, and consequently with our primary duty in reference to ourselves.

THE SENSES

Whenever and wherever we come into contact with our fellow-men, there arises a question of rights, and consequently of duties. We have alluded incidentally to some of them, in speaking of habits and dress. The senses of each individual have their rights, and it is your duty to respect them.

The eye has a claim upon you for so much of beauty in form, color, arrangement, position, and movement as you are able to present to it. A French author has written a book, the aim of which is to show that it is the duty of a pretty woman to look pretty. It is the duty of *all* women, and all men too, to look and behave just as well as they can, and whoever fails in this, fails in good manners and in duty.

The ear demands agreeable tones and harmonious combinations of tones—pleasant words and sweet songs. If you indulge in loud talking, in boisterous and untimely laughter, or in profane or vulgar language, or sing out of tune, you violate its rights and offend good manners.

The sense of smell requires pleasant odors for its enjoyment. Fragrance is its proper element. To bring the fetid odor of unwashed feet or filthy garments, or the stench of bad tobacco—or, worse, whisky—or the offensive scent of onions or garlic within its sphere, is an act of impoliteness.

The sense of taste asks for agreeable flavors, and has a right to the best we can give in the way of palatable foods and drinks.

The sense of feeling, though less cultivated and not so sensitive as the others, has its rights too, and is offended by too great coarseness, roughness, and hardness. It has a claim on us for a higher culture.

The Faculties

And if the senses have their rights, we must admit that the higher faculties and feelings of our nature are at least equally endowed in this respect. You cannot trespass upon one of them without a violation of good manners. We cannot go into a complete exposition of the "bill of rights" of each. You can analyze them for yourself, and learn the nature of their claims upon you. In the meantime, we will touch upon a point or two here and there.

Opinions

Each person has a right to his or her opinions, and to the expression of them *on proper occasions*, and there is no duty more binding upon us all than the most complete and respectful toleration. The author of *The Illustrated Manners Book* truly says:

> "*Every denial of, or interference with, the personal freedom or absolute rights of another, is a violation of good manners.* He who presumes to censure me for my religious belief, or want of belief; who makes it a matter of criticism or reproach that I am a Theist or Atheist, Trinitarian or Unitarian, Catholic or Protestant, Pagan or Christian, Jew, Mohammedan, or Mormon, is guilty of rudeness and insult. If any of these modes of belief makes me intolerant or intru-

sive, he may resent such intolerance or repel such intrusion; but the basis of all true politeness and social enjoyment is the mutual tolerance of personal rights."

The Sacredness of Privacy

Here is another passage from *The Illustrated Manners Book* that is so much to the point that we cannot forbear to copy it:

"One of the rights most commonly trespassed upon constituting a violent breach of good manners, is the right of privacy, or of the control of one's own person and affairs. There are places in this country where there exists scarcely the slightest recognition of this right. A man or woman bolts into your house without knocking. No room is sacred unless you lock the door, and an exclusion would be an insult. Parents intrude upon children, and children upon parents. The husband thinks he has a right to enter his wife's room, and the wife would feel injured if excluded, by night or day, from her husband's. It is said that they even open each other's letters, and claim, as a right, that neither should have any secrets from the other. . . .

"Each person in a dwelling should, if possible, have a room as sacred from intrusion as the house is to the family. No child, grown to years

of discretion, should be outraged by intrusion.
No relation, however intimate, can justify it.
So the trunks, boxes, packets, papers, and letters of every individual, locked or unlocked,
sealed or unsealed, are sacred. It is ill manners
even to open a book, or to read a written paper
lying open, without permission expressed or
implied. . . . Be careful where you go, what you
read, and what you handle, particularly in private apartments."

This right to privacy extends to one's business, his personal
relations, his thoughts, and his feelings. *Don't intrude*; and
always "mind your own business," which means, by implica-
tion, that you must let other people's business alone.

Conformity

You must conform, to such an extent as not to annoy
and give offense, to the customs, whether in dress or other
matters, of the circle in which you move. This conformity is
an implied condition in the social compact. It is a practical
recognition of the rights of others, and shows merely a proper
regard for their opinions and feelings. If you cannot sing in
tune with the rest, or on the same key, remain silent. You
may be right and the others wrong, but that does not alter
the case. Convince them, if you can, and bring them to your
pitch, but never mar even a low accord.

So if you cannot adapt your dress and manners to the company in which you find yourself, the sooner you take your leave
the better. You may and should endeavor, in a proper way, to

change such customs and fashions as you may deem wrong, or injurious in their tendency, but, in the meantime, you have no right to violate them. You may choose your company, but, having chosen it, you must conform to its rules till you can change them. You are not compelled to reside in Rome; but if you choose to live there, you must "do as the Romans do."

The rules that should govern your conduct, as an isolated individual, were such a thing as isolation possible in the midst of society, are modified by your relations to those around you. This life of ours is a complex affair, and our greatest errors arise from our one-sided views of it. We are sovereign individuals, and are born with certain "inalienable rights"; but we are also members of that larger individual society, and our rights cannot conflict with the duties which grow out of that relation. If by means of our nonconformity we cause ourselves to be cut off, like an offending hand, or plucked out, like an offending eye, our usefulness is at once destroyed.

> You may choose your company, but, having chosen it, you must conform to its rules till you can change them.

It is related of a certain king that on a particular occasion he turned his tea into his saucer, contrary to his custom and to the etiquette of society, because two country ladies, whose hospitalities he was enjoying, did so. That king was a *gentleman*; and this anecdote serves to illustrate an important principle; namely, that *true politeness and genuine good manners often not only permit, but absolutely demand, a violation of some of the arbitrary rules of etiquette.*

The *highest law* demands complete HARMONY in all spheres and in all relations.

EQUALITY

In the qualified sense that no doubt Mr. Jefferson affixed to the term in his own mind, "all men *are* created free and *equal.*" The "noble Oracle" himself had long before as explicitly asserted the natural equality of man. In 1739, thirty-seven years before the Declaration of Independence was penned, Lord Chester-field wrote: "We are of the same species, and no distinction whatever is between us, except that which arises from fortune. For example, your footman and Lizette would be your equals were they as rich as you. . . . A good heart never reminds people of their misfortune, but endeavors to alleviate, or, if possible, to make them forget it."

The writer in *Life Illustrated* states the case very clearly as follows:

> "It is in the sacredness of their rights that men are equal. The smallest injustice done to the smallest man on earth is an offense against all men; an offense which all men have a personal and equal interest in avenging. If John Smith picks my pocket, the cause in court is correctly entitled, 'The People *versus* John Smith.' The

whole State of New York has taken up my quarrel with John, and arrays itself against John in awful majesty; because the pockets, the interests, the rights of a man are *infinitely*, and therefore *equally*, sacred.

"The conviction of this truth is the beginning and basis of the science of republican etiquette, which acknowledges no *artificial* distinctions. Its leading principle is that courtesy is due to all men from all men; from the servant to the served; from the served to the servant; and from both for precisely the same reason, namely, because both are human beings and *fellow*-citizens!"

A REMARK OR TWO TO BE REMEMBERED

We purpose, in succeeding chapters, to set forth briefly but clearly what the actual requirements of good society are in reference to behavior. You must look at these in the light of the general principles we have already laid down. It is not for us to say how far you ought or can conform to any particular custom, usage, or rule of etiquette. We believe that even the most arbitrary and capricious of them either have or have had a reason and a meaning. In many cases, however, the reason may no longer exist, and the form is meaningless; or while it embodies what is a living truth to others, you may have outgrown it or advanced beyond it.

You have an undoubted right, politely but firmly, to decline to do what seems to you, looking upon the matter from your highest standpoint, to be clearly wrong, and it is no breach of good manners to do so; but at the same time you should avoid, as far as possible, putting yourself in positions which call for the exercise of this right. If you cannot conscientiously wear a dress coat, or a stove-pipe hat, or cut your hair, or eat meat, or drink wine, you will naturally avoid, under ordinary circumstances, the circles in which nonconformity in these matters would be deemed a breach of good manners.

When it is necessary that you should mingle with people whose customs you cannot follow in all points without a violation of principle, you will courteously, and with proper respect for what they probably think entirely right, fall back upon the "higher law"; but if it is a mere matter of gloved or ungloved hands, cup or saucer, fork or knife, you will certainly have the courtesy and good sense to conform to usage.

Chapter V

DOMESTIC MANNERS

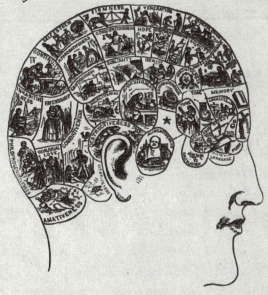

Home is a little world of itself, and furnishes a
sphere for the exercise of every virtue and for the
experience of every pleasure or pain. If one profit
not by its opportunities, he will be likely to pay dearly
for less agreeable lessons in another school.

—Harrison

A TEST OF
GOOD MANNERS

Good manners are not to be put on and off with one's best clothes. Politeness is an article for everyday wear. If you don it only on special and rare occasions, it will be sure to sit awkwardly upon you. If you are not well behaved in your own family circle, you will hardly be truly so anywhere, however strictly you may conform to the observances of good breeding, when in society. The true gentleman or lady is a gentleman or lady at all times and in all places—at home as well as abroad—in the field, or workshop, or in the kitchen, as well as in the parlor. A snob is a *snob* always and everywhere.

If you see a man behave in a rude and uncivil manner to his father or mother, his brothers or sisters, his wife or children; or fail to exercise the common courtesies of life at his own table and around his own fireside, you may at once set him down as a boor, whatever *pretensions* he may make to gentility.

> If you see a man behave in a rude and uncivil manner to his father or mother, his brothers or sisters, his wife or children . . . you may at once set him down as a boor.

Do not fall into the absurd error of supposing that you may do as you please at home—that is, unless you please to behave in a perfectly gentlemanly or ladylike manner. The same rights exist there as elsewhere, and the same duties grow out of them, while the natural respect and affection which should be felt by each member of the family for all the other members add infinitely to their sacredness. Let your good manners, then, begin at home.

CHILDREN

American children (we are sorry to be obliged to say it) are not, as a general rule, well behaved. They are rude and disrespectful, if not disobedient. They inspire terror rather than love in the breasts of strangers and all persons who seek quiet and like order. In our drawing-rooms, on board our steamers, in our railway cars and stagecoaches, they usually contrive to make themselves generally and particularly disagreeable by their familiarity, forwardness, and pertness.

"Young America" cannot brook restraint, has no conception of superiority, and reverences nothing. His ideas of equality admit neither limitation nor qualification. He is born with a full comprehension of his own individual rights, but is slow in learning his social duties. Through whose fault comes this state of things? American boys and girls have naturally as much good sense and good nature as those of any other nation, and, when well trained, no children are more courteous and agreeable. The fault lies in their education. In the days of our grandfathers, children were taught manners at school—a rather rude, backwoods sort of manners, it is true, but better than the no manners at all of the present day.

We must blame parents in this matter rather than their children. If you would have your children grow up beloved and respected by their elders as well as their contemporaries, teach them good manners in their childhood. The young sovereign should first learn to obey, that he may be the better fitted to command in his turn.

> If you would have your children grow up beloved and respected . . . teach them good manners in their childhood.

Those who are old enough to study this book are old enough to take the matter in to their own hands, and remedy the defects and supply the deficiencies of their early education. We beg them to commence at once, and *at home*.

PARENTS

Allow no false ideas of "liberty and equality" to cause you to forget for a moment the deference due to your father and your mother. The fifth commandment has not been and cannot be abrogated. We commend to you the example of the Father of his Country. Look into the life of George Washington, and mark what tender and respectful attentions characterized his intercourse with his only surviving parent. *He* never, we venture to say, spoke of his mother as "the old woman," or addressed her with incivility. "Never," an old friend of yours adjures you, "let youthful levity or the example of others betray you into forgetfulness of the claims of your parents or elders to a certain deference." Nature, a counselor still more sage, we doubt not, has written the same injunction upon your heart. *Let your manners do justice to your feelings!*

The polished and courtly Henry Lunettes, "gentleman of the old school," and the author of the *American Gentleman's Guide to Politeness and Fashion*, says:

> "Toward your father, preserve always a deferential manner, mingled with a certain frankness indicating that thorough confidence—that entire understanding of each other, which is the best guarantee of good sense in both, and of inestimable value to every young man blessed with a right-minded parent. Accept the advice dictated by experience with respect, receive even reproof without impatience of manner, and hasten to prove afterward that you cherish no resentful remembrance of what may have seemed to you too great severity or a too manifest assumption of authority. . . . In the inner temple of *home*, as well as where the world looks on, render him reverence due.

> "There should be mingled with the habitual deference and attention that marks your manner

to your mother the indescribable tenderness and rendering back of care and watchfulness that betokens remembrance of early days. No other woman should ever induce you to forget this truest, most disinterested friend, nor should your manner ever indicate even momentary indifference to her wishes or her affection."

BROTHERS & SISTERS

The intercourse of brothers and sisters should be marked by the frankness and familiarity befitting their intimate relation; but this certainly does not preclude the exercise of all the little courtesies of life.

Young man, be polite to your sister. She is a woman, and all women have claims on you for courteous attentions; and the affection which exists between you adds tenfold to the sacredness of the claims she has upon you, not only for protection, but for the exercise toward her of all the sweet amenities of life. Except your mother and your wife or affianced mistress (if you have one), no one can possibly have an equal right to your attentions. If you are young and have neither wife nor lady-love, let your mother and your sisters be to you the embodiment of all that is tenderest, most beautiful, and best in the human world. You can have no better school than your daily intercourse with them, to fit you for female society in general. The young man who loves his sisters and always treats them with the politeness, deference, and kindness which is their due, is almost certain to be a favorite with their sex generally; so, *as you value your reputation for good manners and your success with other ladies, fail in no act of courtesy to your sisters.*

The gentle and loving sister will need no injunction to treat an affectionate, polite, and attentive brother with the tender and respectful consideration that such a brother deserves. The charming little courtesies that you practice so gracefully in your intercourse with other gentlemen will not, you may be sure, be lost upon him. True politeness is never lost, and never out of place; and nowhere does it appear more attractive than at home.

> The young man who loves his sisters and always treats them with the politeness, deference, and kindness which is their due, is almost certain to be a favorite with their sex generally.

Stiff formality and cold ceremoniousness are repulsive anywhere, and are particularly so in the family circle; but the easy, frank, and genial intercourse of the fireside, instead of being marred, is refined and made still more delightful by courtesy.

THE HUSBAND

Reader, are you married? But excuse us, if the question is not a proper one. If you are not, you doubtless hope to be, sooner or later, and therefore we will address you just as if you were.

The husband should never cease to be a *lover*, or fail in any of those delicate attentions and tender expressions of affectionate solicitude that marked his intercourse before marriage with his heart's queen. All the respectful deference, every courteous observance, all the self-sacrificing devotion that can be claimed by a mistress is certainly due to a wife, and he is no true husband and no true *gentleman* who withholds them.

> [Husbands,] put this honor, respect, and love
> into the forms of speech and action.

It is not enough that you honor, respect, and love your wife. You must put this honor, respect, and love into the forms of speech and action. Let no unkind word, no seeming indifference, no lack of the little attentions due her, remind her sadly of the sweet days of courtship and the honeymoon. Surely the love you thought would have been cheaply purchased at the price of a world is worth all you care to preserve. Is not the wife more, and better, and dearer than the sweetheart? We venture to hint that it is probably your own fault if she is not.

The chosen companion of your life, the mother of your children, the sharer of all your joys and sorrows, as she possesses the highest place in your affections, should have the best place everywhere, the choicest morsels, the politest attentions, the softest, kindest words, the tenderest care. Love, duty, and good manners alike require it.

THE WIFE

And has the wife no duties? Have the courteous observances, the tender watchfulness, the pleasant words, the never-tiring devotion, which won your smiles, your spoken thanks, your kisses, your very self, in days gone by, now lost their value? Does not the husband rightly claim as much, at least, as the lover? If you find him less observant of the little courtesies due you, may this not be because you sometimes fail to reward him with the same sweet thanks and sweeter smiles? Ask your own heart.

> **Have the comfort and happiness of your husband always in view, and let him *see* and *feel* that you still look up to him with trust and affection.**

Have the comfort and happiness of your husband always in view, and let him *see* and *feel* that you still look up to him with trust and affection—that the love of other days has not grown cold. Dress for his eyes more scrupulously than for all the rest of the world; make yourself and your home beautiful for his sake; play and sing (if you can) to please him; try to beguile him from his cares; retain his affections in the same way you won them, and—be polite even to your husband.

ENTERTAINERS & THEIR GUESTS

Hospitality takes a high rank among the social virtues; but we fear it is not held in so high esteem as formerly. Its duties are often fatiguing and irksome, no doubt, and sometimes quite unnecessarily so. One of the most important maxims of hospitality is, "Let your guests alone!" If it were generally observed it would save both hosts and visitors a world of trouble. Your first object should be to make your guests feel at home. This they never can do while your needless bustle and obtrusive attentions constantly remind them that they are not at home, and perhaps make them wish they were.

> Your first object should be
> to make your guests feel at home.

You will not, of course, understand us to mean that you should devote no attention to your guests. On the contrary, you should assiduously labor to promote their comfort and enjoyment, opening to them every source of entertainment within your reach; but it should be done in that easy, delicate, considerate way which will make it seem a matter of course, and no trouble whatever to you. You should not seem to be conferring but receiving a favor.

Begging your visitors to "make themselves at home," does not give them the home *feeling*. Genuine, unaffected friendliness, and an unobtrusive and almost unperceived attention to their wants alone will impart this. Allow their presence to interfere as little as possible with your domestic arrangements; thus letting them see that their visit does not disturb you, but that they fall, as it were, naturally into a vacant place in your household.

Observe your own feelings when you happen to be the guest of a person who, though he may be very much your friend, and really glad to see you, seems not to know what to do either with you or himself; and again, when in the house of another, you feel as much at ease as in your own. Mark the difference, more easily felt than described, between the manners of the two, and deduce therefrom a lesson for your own improvement.

Furnish your rooms and table for your guests in as good style as your means and the circumstances of the case will permit, and make no fuss about it. To be unnecessarily sparing shows meanness, and to be extravagantly profuse is absurd as well as ruinous. Probably your visitors know whether your income is large or small and if they do not they will soon learn, on that point, all that it is necessary for them to know. But if any circumstance out of the ordinary course of things should render an apology necessary, make it at once and say no more about it.

Avoid by all means the very common but very foolish habit of depreciating your own rooms, furniture, or food, and expressing uncalled-for regrets that you have nothing better to offer, merely to give your guests an opportunity politely to contradict you. But you need not go to the other extreme and extol the meats you set before them. Say nothing about these matters.

> Avoid . . . the very common but very foolish habit of depreciating your own rooms, furniture, or food, and expressing uncalled-for regrets that you have nothing better to offer.

When visitors show any intention of leaving, you will of course express the desire you feel to have them stay longer, but good manners do not require you to endeavor to retain them against their wishes or sense of duty. It is to be supposed that they know their own affairs best.

Guests sometimes forget (if they ever learned) that *they* have any duties. We beg leave to jog their memory with the following hints from the graceful pen of "Mrs. Manners":

> "To accommodate yourself to the habits and
> rules of the family, in regard to hours of rising
> or retiring, and particularly the hours for meals,
> is the first duty of a guest. Inform yourself
> as soon as possible when the meals occur—

whether there will be a dressing-bell—at what time they meet for prayers, and thus become acquainted with all the family regulations. *It is always the better way for a family to adhere strictly to all their usual habits*; it is a much simpler matter for one to learn to conform to those than for half a dozen to be thrown out of a routine, which may be almost indispensable to the fulfillment of their importunate duties. It certainly must promote the happiness of any reasonable person to know that his presence is no restraint and no inconvenience.

"Your own good sense and delicacy will teach you the desirability of keeping your room tidy, and your articles of dress and toilet as much in order as possible. If there is a deficiency of servants, a lady will certainly not hesitate to make her own bed, and to do for herself as much as possible, and for the family all that is in her power."

SERVANTS

We are all dependent, in one way or another, upon others. At one time we serve, at another we are served, and we are equally worthy of honor and respect in the one case as in the other. The man or the woman who serves us may or may not be our inferior in natural capacity, learning, manners, or wealth. Be this as it may, the relation in which we stand to him or her gives us no right beyond the exaction of the service stipulated or implied in that relation. The right to tyrannize over our inferiors in social position, to unnecessarily humiliate them, or to be rude and unkind cannot exist, because it would be an infringement of others rights. Servants have rights as well as those whom they serve, and the latter have duties as well as the former. We owe those who labor for us something more than their wages. They have claims on us for a full recognition of their manhood or womanhood, and all the rights that grow out of that state.

> It is a small thing to say, "I thank you," but those little words are often better than gold.

The true gentleman is never arrogant, or overbearing, or rude to domestics or employees. His commands are requests, and all services, no matter how humble the servant, are received with thanks, as if they were favors. We might say the same with still greater emphasis of the true lady. There is no surer sign of vulgarity than a needless assumption of the tone of authority and a haughty and supercilious bearing toward servants and inferiors in station generally. It is a small thing to say, "I thank you," but those little words are often better than gold. No one is too poor to bestow, or too rich to receive them.

CHAPTER VI

THE OBSERVANCES OF EVERYDAY LIFE

*Good manners are the settled medium of social,
as specie is of commercial life: returns are equally expected
in both; and people will no more advance their civility to
a bear, than their money to a bankrupt.*

—LORD CHESTERFIELD

A PRELIMINARY REMARK

. . .We shall now essay a brief exposition of the established laws of etiquette, leaving each reader to judge for himself how far he can and ought to conform to them, and what modifications they require to adapt them to a change of time, place, and circumstances.

INTRODUCTIONS

It is neither necessary nor desirable to introduce everybody to everybody; and the promiscuous presentations sometimes inflicted upon us are anything but agreeable. You confer no favor on us, and only a nominal one on the person presented, by making us acquainted with one whom we do not desire to know; and you *may* inflict a positive injury upon both. You also put yourself in an unpleasant position; for "an introduction is a social endorsement," and will become to a certain extent responsible for the person you introduce. If he disgraces himself in any way, you share, in a greater or less degree, in his disgrace. Be as cautious in this matter. . . .

As a general rule, no gentleman should be presented to a lady without her permission being previously obtained.

Between gentlemen this formality is not always necessary, but you should have good reason to believe that the acquaintance will be agreeable to both, before introducing any persons to each other. If a gentleman requests you to present him to another gentleman who is his superior in social position, or to a lady, you should either obtain permission of the latter, or decline to accede to his request, on the ground that you are not sufficiently intimate yourself to take the liberty.

If you are walking with a friend, and are met or joined by another, it is not necessary to introduce them to each other; but you may do so if you think they would be glad to become acquainted. The same rule will apply to other accidental meetings.

When two men call upon a stranger on a matter of business, each should present the other.

The inferior should be introduced to the superior—the gentleman to the lady, as, "Miss Brown, permit me to introduce Mr. Smith." A lady may, however, be introduced to a gentleman much her superior in age or station. Gentlemen and ladies who are presumed to be equals in age and position are mutually introduced; as, "Mr. Wilson, allow me to make you acquainted with Mr. Parker; Mr. Parker, Mr. Wilson."

> The inferior should be introduced to the superior . . .
> a lady may, however, be introduced to a gentleman
> much her superior in age or station.

In presenting persons, be very careful to speak their names plainly; and on being introduced to another, if you do not catch the name, say, without hesitation or embarrassment, "I beg your pardon, I did not hear the name."

It is the common custom in this country to shake hands on being introduced. It is better that this should be optional with the person to whom you are presented or with you, if you stood in the position of the superior. If a lady or a superior in age or social position offers the hand, you of course accept it cordially. You will have too much self-respect to be the first to extend the hand in such a case. In merely formal introductions a bow is enough. Feeling should govern in this matter.

> If a lady or a superior in age or social position offers the hand, you of course accept it cordially.

In introducing members of your own family, you should always mention their name. Say, "My father Mr. Jones," "My daughter Miss Jones," or "Miss Mary Jones." Your wife is simply "Mrs. Jones"; and if there happen to be another Mrs. Jones in the family, she may be "Mrs. Jones, my sister-in-law," etc. To speak of your wife as "my lady," or enter yourselves on a hotel register as Mr. Jones and lady, is particularly *snobbish*.

Introductions by letter are subject to the same general rules as verbal ones: we should, however, be still more cautious in giving them.

But may we not speak to a person without an introduction? In many cases we most certainly may and should. There is no reason in the world why two persons who may occupy the same seat in a railway car or a stagecoach should remain silent during the whole journey because they have not been introduced, when conversation might be agreeable to both. The same remark will apply to many other occasions. You are not obliged, however, to know these *extempore* acquaintances afterward.

If you are a gentleman, do not, we beg you, permit the lack of an introduction to prevent you from promptly offering your services to any unattended lady who may need them. Take off your hat and politely beg the honor of protecting, escorting, or assisting her, and when the service has been accomplished, bow and retire.

SALUTATIONS

"Salutation," a French writer says, "is the touchstone of good breeding." Your good sense will teach you that it should vary in style with persons, times, places, and circumstances. You will meet an intimate friend with a hearty shake of the hand and an inquiry indicative of real interest, in reference to his health and that of his family. To another person you bow respectfully without speaking. A slight note of recognition suffices in another case. But you should never come into the presence of any person, unless you feel at liberty to ignore their existence altogether, without some form of salutation. If you meet in company a person with whom you have a quarrel, it is better in general to bow coldly and ceremoniously than to seem not to see him.

It is a great rudeness not to return a salutation, no matter how humble the person who salutes you. "A bow," La Fontaine says, "is a note drawn at sight. If you acknowledge it, you must pay the full amount." The two best-bred men in England, Charles the Second and George the Fourth, never failed to take off their hats to the meanest of their subjects. A greater man than either, and a true "gentleman of the old school," George Washington, was wont to lift his hat even to the poor . . . slave, who took off his as that great man passed.

> It is a great rudeness not to return a salutation, no matter how humble the person who salutes you.

RECEIVING VISITORS

The duty of receiving visitors usually devolves upon the mistress of the house, and should be performed in an easy, quiet, and self-possessed manner, and without any unnecessary ceremony. In this way you will put your guests at their ease, and make their call or visit pleasant both to them and to yourself. From a little book before us entitled *Etiquette for Ladies*, we condense a few useful hints on this subject:

"When any one enters, whether announced or not, rise immediately, advance toward him, and request him to sit down. If it is a young man, *offer* him an arm-chair, or a stuffed one; if an elderly man, *insist* upon his *accepting* the arm-chair; if a lady, beg her to be seated upon the sofa. If the master of the house receives the visitors, he will take a chair and place himself at a little distance from them; if, on the contrary, it is the mistress of the house, and if she is intimate with the lady who visits her, she will place herself near her. If several ladies come at once, we give the most honorable place to the one who, from age or other considerations, is most entitled to respect. In winter, the most honorable places are those at the corners of the fireplace.

"If the visitor is a stranger, the master or mistress of the house rises, and any persons who may be already in the room should do the same. If some of them then withdraw, the master or mistress of the house should conduct them as far as the door. But whoever the person may be who departs, if we have other company, we may dispense with conducting farther than the door of the room."

Quiet self-possession and unaffected courtesy will enable you to make even a ceremonious morning call tolerable, if not absolutely pleasant to both the caller and yourself.

VISITS & CALLS

Visits are of various kinds, each of which has its own terms and observances. There are visits of ceremony, visits of congratulation, visits of condolence, visits of friendship:

- Visits of ceremony, though they take up a large share of the time of the fashionable lady, are very stupid affairs as a general thing, and have little to recommend them except—Fashion. The best thing about them is that they may and should be short.
- You pay visits of congratulation to your friends on the occurrence of any particularly auspicious event in his family, or on his appointment to any office or dignity.
- Visits of condolence should be made within the week after the event that calls for them.
- Let visits of friendship be governed by friendship's own laws, and the universal principles of good manners. We shall give no particular rules for the regulation of their time or their length.

"Morning calls," *The Illustrated Manners Book* says, "are the small change of social commerce; parties and assemblies are the heavy drafts. A call is not less than ten nor more than twenty minutes in the city; in the country a little longer. The time for a morning call is between eleven and two o'clock, unless your friends are so fashionable as to dine at five or six, in which case you can call from twelve to three. Morning, in fashionable parlance, means any time before dinner."

In a morning call or visit of ceremony, the gentleman takes his hat and cane, if he carries one, into the room. The lady does not take off her bonnet and shawl. In attending ladies who are making morning calls, a gentleman assists them up the steps, rings the bell, *follows* them into the room, and waits till they have finished their salutations, unless he has a part to perform in presenting them. Ladies should always be the first to rise in leaving a house, and when they have made their *adieux*, their cavaliers repeat the ceremony, and follow them out.

According to Henry Lunettes, soiled overshoes or wet garments should not be worn into any room devoted to the use of ladies. Gentlemen must never remain seated in the company of ladies with whom he is ceremoniously associated, while they are standing. Always relieve ladies of their parcels, parasols, shawls, etc. whenever this will conduce to their convenience.

If you call on a person who is "engaged," or "not at home," leave your card. If there are several persons you desire to see, leave a card for each, or desire a servant to present your compliments to them severally. All visits should be returned, personally or by card, just as one should speak when spoken to, or answer a respectful letter.

According to *The Illustrated Manners Book*, in visiting at a hotel, do not enter your friend's room till your card has announced you. If not at home, send your card to his room with your address written upon it as well as the name of the person for whom it is intended, to avoid mistakes.

Etiquette for Gentlemen offers advice on taking leave. When you are going abroad, intending to be absent for some time, you enclose your card in an envelope, having first written T. T. L. [to take leave] or P. P. C. [*pour prendre congé*] upon it—for a man the former is better—and direct it outside to the person for whom it is intended. In taking leave of a *family*, you send as many cards as you would if you were paying an ordinary visit. When you return from your voyage, all the persons to whom, before going, you have sent cards, will pay you the first visit. If, previously to a voyage or his marriage, any one should not send his card to another, it is to be understood that he wishes the acquaintance to cease. The person, therefore, who is thus *dis*carded, should never again visit the other.

Visiting cards should be engraved or handsomely written. . . . A gentleman's card should be of medium size, unglazed, ungilt, and perfectly plain. A lady's card may be larger and finer, and should be carried in a card-case.

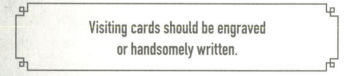

Visiting cards should be engraved or handsomely written.

If you should happen to be paying an evening visit at a house, where, unknown to you, there is a small party assembled, you should enter and present yourself precisely as you would have done had you been invited. To retire precipitately with an apology for the intrusion would create a *scene*, and be extremely awkward. Go in, therefore, converse with ease for a few moments, and then retire.

In making morning calls, usage allows a gentleman to wear a frock coat, or a sack coat, if the latter happen to be in fashion. The frock coat is now, in this country, *tolerated* at dinner-parties, and even at a ball, but is not considered in good . . . style.

APPOINTMENTS

Be exact in keeping all appointments. It is better never to avail yourself of even the quarter of an hour's grace sometimes allowed.

If you make an appointment with another at your own house, you should be invisible to the rest of the world, and consecrate your time solely to him.

If you accept an appointment at the house of a public officer or a man of business, be very punctual, transact the affair with dispatch, and retire the moment it is finished.

At a dinner or supper to which you have accepted an invitation, be absolutely punctual. It is very annoying to arrive an hour before the rest, and still worse to be too late. If you find yourself in the latter predicament on an occasion where ceremony is required, send in your card, with an apology, and retire.

TABLE MANNERS

We shall speak in another place of the ceremonious observances requisite at formal dinner parties. Our observations here will be of a more general character, and of universal application.

- Take your seat quietly at the table. Sit firmly in your chair, without lolling, leaning back, drumming, or any other uncouth action.
- Unfold your napkin and lay it in your lap.
- Eat soup delicately with a spoon, holding a piece of bread in your left hand. Be careful to make no noise in chewing or swallowing your food.
- Cut your food with your knife; but the fork is to be used to convey it to your mouth. A spoon is employed for food that cannot be eaten with a fork. Take your fork or spoon in the right hand. Never use both hands to convey anything to your mouth.
- Break your bread, not cut or bite it.
- Your cup was made to drink from, and your saucer to hold the cup. It is not well to drink anything hot; but you can wait till your tea or coffee cools.
- Eggs should be eaten from the shell (chipping off a little of the *larger* end), with or without an egg-cup. The egg-cup is to hold the shell, and not its contents.

- Be attentive to the wants of any lady who may be seated next to you, especially where there are no servants, and pass anything that may be needful to others.
- When you send up your plate for anything, your knife and fork should go with it.
- When you have finished the course, lay your knife and fork on your plate, parallel to each other, with the handles toward your right hand.
- Of course, you should never put your knife into the butter or the salt, or your spoon into the sugar-bowl.
- *Eat moderately and slowly*, for your health's sake; but rapid, gross, and immoderate eating is as vulgar as it is unwholesome.
- Never say or do anything at table that is liable to produce disgust. Wipe your nose, if needful, but never blow it. If it is necessary to do this, or to spit, leave the table.
- It is almost unnecessary to mention that the tablecloth is not the place to put your salt. Bread is the only comestible which the custom of well-bred people permits to be laid off your plate.
- It is well not to seem too much in haste to commence, as if you are famishing, but neither is it necessary to wait till everybody is served before you commence.
- It is perfectly proper to "take the last piece," if you want it, always presuming that there is more of the same in reserve.

CONVERSATIONS

As conversation is the principal business in company, we cannot well pay too much attention to it; . . . The maxims that follow are mostly compiled from other works now before us.

According to Jean de La Bruyère, the wit of conversation consists more in finding it in others than in showing a great deal yourself. He who goes from your conversation pleased with himself and his own wit, is perfectly well pleased with you. The most delicate pleasure is to please another.

> Talk to a mother about her children. Women are never tired of hearing of themselves and their children.

According to *Etiquette for Gentlemen*, men of all sorts of occupations meet in society. As they go there to unbend their minds and escape from the fetters of business, you should never, in an evening, speak to a man about his profession. Do not talk of politics to a journalist, of fevers to a physician, of stocks to a broker. Talk to a mother about her children. Women are never tired of hearing of themselves and their children.

In promiscuous companies, you should vary your address agreeably to the different ages of the persons to whom you speak. It would be rude and absurd to talk of your courtships or your pleasures to men of certain dignity and gravity, to clergymen, or men in years. To women you should always address yourself with great respect and attention; their sex is entitled to it, and it is among the duties of good manners; at the same time, that respect is very properly and very agreeably mixed with a degree of gaiety, if you have it.

In relating anything, avoid repetitions, or very hackneyed expressions, such as, *says he*, or *says she*. Some people will use these so often as to take off the hearer's attention from the story; as, in an organ out of tune, one pipe shall perhaps sound the whole time we are playing, and confuse the piece so as not to be understood.

Carefully avoid talking either of your own or other people's domestic concerns. By doing the one, you will be thought vain; by entering into the other, you will be considered officious. Talking of yourself is an impertinence to the company; your affairs are nothing to them; besides, they cannot be kept too secret. As to the affairs of others, what are they to you?

> **Talking of yourself is an impertinence to the company; your affairs are nothing to them.**

You should never help out or forestall the slow speaker, as if you alone were rich in expressions, and he were poor. You may take it for granted that everyone is vain enough to think he can talk well, though he may modestly deny it. [There is an exception to this rule. In speaking with foreigners, who understand our language imperfectly, and may be unable to find the right word, it is sometimes polite to assist them by suggesting the word they require.]

Giving advice unasked is another piece of rudeness. It is, in effect, declaring ourselves wiser than those to whom we give it;

reproaching them with ignorance and inexperience. It is a freedom that ought not to be taken with any common acquaintance.

> Giving advice unasked is another piece of rudeness.

Those who contradict others upon all occasions, and make every assertion a matter of dispute, betray, by this behavior, a want of acquaintance with good breeding.

Vulgarism in language is the next and distinguishing characteristic of bad company and a bad education. A man of fashion avoids nothing with more care than that. As Lord Chesterfield noted, proverbial expressions and trite sayings are the flowers of the rhetoric of a vulgar man.

Never descend to flattery; but deserved compliments should never be withheld. Be attentive to any person who may be speaking to you, and be equally ready to speak or to listen, as the case may require. Never dispute. As a general rule, do not ride your own *hobbies* in a mixed company, nor allow yourself to be "trotted out" for their amusement.

MUSIC

When music commences, conversation should cease. It is very rude to talk while another person is singing or playing.

A lady should never exhibit any anxiety to sing or play; but if she intends to do so, she should not affect to refuse when asked, but obligingly accede at once. If you cannot sing, or do not choose to, say so with seriousness and gravity, and put an end to the expectation promptly. After singing once or twice, cease and give place to others. The complaint is as old as the days of Horace, that a singer can with the greatest difficulty be set agoing, and when agoing, cannot be stopped.

In playing an accompaniment for another, do not forget that it is intended to aid, and not to interrupt, and that the instrument is subordinate to the singer.

When a lady is playing, it is desirable that someone should turn the sheet music for her. Some gentleman will be generally at hand to do this, but unless he is able to read music, his services may as well be dispensed with.

MISCELLANEOUS HINTS

WHICH GOES FIRST?

In ascending or descending stairs with a lady, it is proper to offer your arm, provided the staircase is sufficiently wide to permit two to go up or down abreast.

But if it is not, which should go first? Authorities disagree. Usage is not settled. It is a general rule of etiquette to give ladies the precedence everywhere. Is there a sufficient reason for making this an exception? One says that if you follow a lady in going down stairs, you are liable to tread on her dress, and that if she precedes you in going up, she might display a large foot or a thick ankle that were better concealed. He thinks the gentleman should go first. Another calls this a maxim of prudery and the legacy of a maiden aunt.

> **It is a general rule of etiquette to give ladies the precedence everywhere.**

Colonel Lunettes, our oft-quoted friend of the old *régime*, speaks very positively on this point. "Nothing is more absurd," he says, "than the habit of preceding ladies in ascending stairs, adopted by some men—as if by following just behind them, as one should if the arm be disengaged, there can be any impropriety. Soiled frills and unmended hose must have originated this vulgarity." Let the ladies decide.

An American Habit

There is a habit peculiar to the United States, and from which even some females, who class themselves as ladies, are not entirely free—that of lolling back, balanced upon the two hind legs of a chair. Such a breach of good breeding is rarely committed in Europe. Lolling is carried even so far in America, that it is not uncommon to see the attorneys lay their feet upon the council table; and the clerks and judges theirs also upon their desks in open court.

Gloved or Ungloved?

In shaking hands, it is more respectful to offer an ungloved hand; but if two gentlemen are both gloved, it is very foolish to keep each other waiting to take them off. You should not, however, offer a gloved hand to a lady or a superior who is ungloved. Foreigners are sometimes very sensitive in this matter, and might deem the glove an insult. It is well for a gentleman to carry his right-hand glove in his hand where he is likely to have occasion to shake hands. At a ball or a party the gloves should not be taken off.

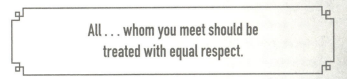

All . . . whom you meet should be treated with equal respect.

Equality

In company, though none are *free*, yet all are *equal*. All, therefore, whom you meet should be treated with equal respect, although interest may dictate toward each different degrees of attention. It is disrespectful to the inviter to shun any of her guests.

Pulling out One's Watch

Pulling out your watch in company, unasked, either at home or abroad, is a mark of ill-breeding. If at home, it appears as if you were tired of your company, and wished them to be gone; if abroad, as if the hours dragged heavily, and you wished to be gone yourself.

If you want to know the time, withdraw; besides, as the taking what is called French leave was introduced, that, on one person's leaving the company, the rest might not be disturbed, looking at your watch does what that piece of politeness was designed to prevent.

Husband and Wife

A gentleman speaks of his wife in a mixed company as Mrs. ——, and a lady of her husband as Mr. ——. So one does not say in speaking to another, "your wife," or "your husband," but Mrs. or Mr. ——. Among intimates, however, to say "my wife," or "my husband," is better, because less formal. Let there be a *fitness* in everything, whatever conventional rules you may violate.

Bowing vs. Curtseying

Curtseying is obsolete. Ladies now universally bow instead. The latter is certainly a more convenient, if not a more graceful form of salutation, particularly on the street.

Presents

Among friends, presents ought to be made of things of small value; or, if valuable, their worth should be derived from the style of the workmanship, or from some accidental circumstance, rather than from the inherent and solid richness. Especially never offer to a lady a gift of great cost; it is in the highest degree indelicate, and looks as if you were desirous of placing her under an obligation to you, and of buying her goodwill.

The gifts made by ladies to gentlemen are of the most refined nature possible; they should be little articles not purchased, but deriving a priceless value as being the offspring of their gentle skill; a little picture from their pencil or a trifle from their needle.

> **A present should be made with as little parade and ceremony as possible.**

A present should be made with as little parade and ceremony as possible. If it is a small matter, a gold pencil-case, a thimble to a lady, or an affair of that sort, it should not be offered formally, but in an indirect way.

Emerson says: "Rings and other jewels are not gifts, but apologies for gifts. The only gift is a portion of thyself. Thou must bleed for me. Therefore the poet brings his poem; the shepherd, his lamb; the farmer, his corn; the miner, a gem; the sailor, coral and shells; the painter, his picture; the girl, a handkerchief of her own sewing."

SNOBBERY

When you hear a man insisting upon points of etiquette and fashion—wondering, for instance, how people can eat with steel forks and survive it, or what charms existence has for persons who dine at three without soup and fish—be sure that that individual is a snob.

CHILDREN

Show, but do not show off, your children to strangers. Recollect, in the matter of children, how many are born every hour, each almost as remarkable as yours in the eyes of its papa and mamma.

Show, but do not show off, your children to strangers.

Chapter VII

THE ETIQUETTE OF OCCASIONS

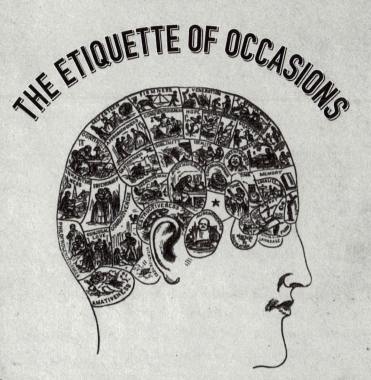

Great plenty, much formality, small cheer,
And everybody out of his own sphere.

—Lord Byron

DINNER PARTIES

A young man or a young woman, unaccustomed to the settled observances of such occasions, can hardly pass through a severer ordeal than a formal dinner. Its terrors, however, are often greatly magnified. Such a knowledge of the principal points of table etiquette as you may acquire from this book, complete self-possession, habits of observation, and a fair share of practical good sense, will carry one safely if not pleasantly through it.

You may entertain the opinion that such dinners, and formal parties in general, are tiresome affairs, and that there might be quite as much real courtesy and a great deal more enjoyment with less ceremony, and we may entirely agree with you; but what *is*, and not what *might be*, is the point to be elucidated. We are to take society as we find it.

[The dinner party's] terrors . . .
are often greatly magnified.

You may, as a general rule, decline invitations to dinner parties without any breach of good manners, and without giving offense, if you think that neither your enjoyment nor your interests will be promoted by accepting; or you may not go into what is technically called "society" at all, and yet you are liable, at a hotel, on board a steamer, or on some extraordinary occasion, to be placed in a position in which ignorance of dinner etiquette will be very mortifying and the information contained in this section be worth a hundred times the cost of the book.

We now proceed to note the common routine of a fashionable dinner, as laid down in books and practiced in polite society. On some points usage is not uniform, but varies in different countries, and even in different cities in the same country, as well as in different circles in the same place. For this reason you must not rely wholly upon this or any other manners book, but, keeping your eyes open and your wits about you, *wait and see what others do*, and follow the prevailing mode.

INVITATIONS

Invitations to a dinner are usually issued several days before the appointed time—the length of time being proportioned to the grandeur of the occasion. On receiving one, you should answer at once, addressing the lady of the house. You should either accept or decline unconditionally, as they will wish to know whom to expect, and make their preparations accordingly.

DRESS

You must go to a dinner party in "full dress." Just what this is, is a question of time and place. Strictly interpreted, it allows gentlemen but little choice. A black dress coat and trousers, a black or white vest and cravat, white gloves, and pumps and silk stockings were formerly rigorously insisted upon. But the freedom-loving "spirit of the age" has already made its influence felt even in the realms of fashion, and a little more latitude is now allowed in most circles.

The American Gentleman's Guide enumerates the essentials of a gentleman's dress for occasions of ceremony in general, as follows:

> "A stylish, well-fitting cloth coat, of some dark color and of unexceptionable quality, nether garments to correspond, or in warm weather, or under other suitable circumstances, white pants of a fashionable material and make, the finest and purest linen, embroidered in white, if at all; a cravat and vest of some dark or neutral tint, according to the physiognomical peculiarities of the wearer and the *prevailing mode*; an entirely fresh-looking, fashionable black hat, and carefully fitted modish boots, white gloves, and a soft, thin, white handkerchief."

A lady's "full dress" is not easily defined, and fashion allows her greater scope for the exercise of her taste in the selection of materials, the choice of colors, and the style of making. Still, she must "be in the fashion."

PUNCTUALITY

Never allow yourself to be a minute behind the time. The dinner cannot be served till all the guests have arrived. If it is spoiled through your tardiness, you are responsible not only to your inviter, but to his outraged guests. Better be too late for the steamer or the railway train than for a dinner!

GOING TO THE TABLE

When dinner is announced, the host rises and requests all to walk to the dining-room, to which he leads the way, having given his arm to the lady who, from age or any other consideration, is entitled to precedence. Each gentleman offers his arm to a lady, and all follow in order. If you are not the principal guest, you must be careful not to offer your arm to the handsomest or most distinguished lady.

ARRANGEMENT OF GUESTS

Where rank or social position is regarded (and where are they not to some extent?), the two most distinguished gentlemen are placed next to the mistress of the house, and the two most distinguished ladies next to the master of the house. The right hand is especially the place of honor. If it is offered to you, you should not refuse it.

> The right hand is especially the place of honor. If it is offered to you, you should not refuse it.

It is one of the first and most difficult things properly to arrange the guests, and to place them in such a manner that the conversation may always be general during the entertainment. If the number of gentlemen is nearly equal to that of the ladies, we should take care to intermingle them. We should separate husbands from their wives, and remove near relations as far from one another as possible, because being always together they ought not to converse among themselves in a general party.

Duties of the Host

To perform faultlessly the honors of the table is one of the most difficult things in society; it might indeed be asserted, without much fear of contradiction, that no man has as yet ever reached exact propriety in his office as host. When he receives others, he must be content to forget himself; he must relinquish all desire to shine, and even all attempts to please his guests by conversation, and rather do all in his power to let them please one another.

Help ladies with a due appreciation of their delicacy, moderation, and fastidiousness of their appetites; and do not overload the plate of any person you serve. Never pour gravy on a plate without permission. It spoils the meat for some persons.

> Do not overload the plate of any person you serve.

Do not insist upon your guests partaking of particular dishes; never ask persons more than once, and never put anything by force upon their plates. It is extremely ill-bred, though extremely common, to press one to eat of anything.

The host should never recommend or eulogize any particular dish; his guests will take it for granted that anything found at his table is excellent.

The most important maxim in hospitality is to leave everyone to his own choice and enjoyment, and to free him *from an ever-present sense of being entertained*. You should never send away your own plate until all your guests have finished.

Duties of the Guests

Gentlemen must be assiduous but not officious in their attentions to the ladies. See that they lack nothing, but do not seem to watch them.

If a "grace" is to be asked, treat the observance with respect. Good manners require this, even if veneration fails to suggest it.

- Soup: Soup will come first. *You must not decline it*; because nothing else can be served till the first course is finished, and to sit with nothing before you would be awkward. But you may eat as little of it as you choose. The host serves his left-hand neighbor first, then his right hand, and so on till all are served. Take whatever is given you, and do *not* offer it to your neighbor; and begin at once to eat. You must not suck soup into your mouth, blow it, or send for a second plate.
- Fish: The second course is fish, which is to be eaten with a fork, and without vegetables. The last part of this injunction does not, of course, apply to informal dinners, where fish is the principal dish. Fish, like soup, is served but once. When you have eaten what you wish, you lay your fork on your plate, and the waiter removes it.
- Meats/Side Dishes: The third course brings the principal dishes—roast and boiled meats, fowl, etc., which are followed by game. There are also side dishes of various kinds.

- Dessert: At dessert, help the ladies near you to whatever they may require. Serve strawberries with a spoon, but pass cherries, grapes, or peaches for each to help himself with his fingers. You need not volunteer to pare an apple or a peach for a lady, but should do so, of course, at her request, using her fork or some other than your own to hold it.

We have said in our remarks on table manners in general, in a previous chapter, that in sending your plate for anything, you should leave your knife and fork upon it. For this injunction we have the authority of most of the books on etiquette, as well as of general usage. There seems also to be a reason for the custom in the fact that to hold them in your hand would be awkward, and to lay them on the tablecloth might soil it; but the author of the *American Gentleman's Guide*, whose acquaintance with the best usage is not to be questioned, says that they should be retained, and either kept together in the hand, or rested upon your bread, to avoid soiling the cloth.

Eat deliberately and decorously (there can be no harm in repeating this precept), masticate your food thoroughly, and *beware of drinking too much ice-water*.

If your host is not a "temperance man," that is, one pledged to total abstinence, wine will probably be drunk. You can of course decline, but you must do so courteously, and without any reflection upon those who drink. You are not invited to deliver a temperance lecture.

Where finger-glasses are used, dip the tips of your fingers in the water and wipe them on your napkin; and wet a corner of the napkin and wipe your mouth. Snobs sometimes wear gloves at table. It is not necessary that you should imitate them.

The French fashion of having the principal dishes carved on a side-table, and served by attendants, is now very generally adopted at ceremonious dinners in this country, but few gentlemen who go into company at all can safely count upon never being called upon to carve, and the *art* is well worth acquiring. Ignorance of it sometimes places one in an awkward position. You will find directions on this subject in almost any cookbook; you will learn more, however, by watching an accomplished carver than in any other way.

> **Snobs sometimes wear gloves at table. It is not necessary that you should imitate them.**

Do not allow yourself to be too much engrossed in attending to the wants of the stomach to join in the cheerful interchange of civilities and thoughts with those near you.

We must leave a hundred little things connected with a dinner party unmentioned; but what we have said here, together with the general canons of eating laid down in a section of Chapter VI ("Table Manners"), and a little observation, will soon make you proficient in the etiquette of these occasions, in which, if you will take our advice, you will not participate very frequently.

An *informal* dinner, at which you meet two or three friends, and find more cheer and less ceremony, is much to be preferred.

EVENING PARTIES

Evening parties are of various kinds, and more or less ceremonious, as they are more or less fashionable. Their object is or should be social enjoyment, and the manners of the company ought to be such as will best promote it. A few hints, therefore, in addition to the general maxims of good behavior already laid down, will suffice.

INVITATIONS

Having accepted an invitation to a party, never fail to keep your promise, and especially do not allow bad weather, of any ordinary character, to prevent your attendance. A married man should never accept an invitation from a lady in which his wife is not included.

> A married man should never accept an invitation from a lady in which his wife is not included.

SALUTATIONS

According to *Etiquette for Gentlemen*, when you enter a drawing-room where there is a party, you salute the lady of the house before speaking to anyone else. Even your most intimate friends are enveloped in an opaque atmosphere until you have made your bow to your entertainer. You then mix with the company, salute your acquaintances, and join in the conversation. You may converse freely with any person you meet on such an occasion, without the formality of an introduction.

Conversation

When conversation is not general, nor the subject sufficiently interesting to occupy the whole company, they break up into different groups. Each one converses with one or more of his neighbors on his right and left. We should, if we wish to speak to anyone, avoid leaning upon the person who happens to be between. According to Madame Élisabeth Celnart, a gentleman ought not to lean upon the arm of a lady's chair, but he may, if standing, support himself by the back of it, in order to converse with the lady partly turned toward him.

The members of an invited family should never be seen conversing with one another at a party.

French Leave

If you desire to withdraw before the party breaks up, take "French leave"—that is, go quietly out without disturbing anyone, and without saluting even the mistress of the house, unless you can do so without attracting attention. The contrary course would interrupt the rest of the company, and call for otherwise unnecessary explanations and ceremony.

Sports and Games

Among young people, and particularly in the country, a variety of sports or plays, as they are called, are in vogue. Some of them are fitting only for children; but others are more intellectual, and may be made sources of improvement as well as of amusement.

Entering into the spirit of these sports, we throw off some of the restraints of a more formal intercourse; but they furnish no excuse for rudeness. You must not forget your politeness in your hilarity, or allow yourself to "take liberties," or lose your sense of delicacy and propriety.

The selection of the games or sports belongs to the ladies, though any person may modestly propose any amusement, and ask the opinion of others in reference to it. The person who gives the party will exercise her prerogative to vary the play, that the interest may be kept up.

> You must not forget your politeness in your hilarity, or allow yourself to "take liberties."

If this were the proper place, we should enter an earnest protest against the promiscuous kissing which sometimes forms part of the performances in some of these games, but it is not our office to proscribe or introduce observances, but to regulate them. No true gentleman will *abuse* the freedom which the laws of the game allows; but if required, will delicately kiss the hand, the forehead, or, at most, the cheek of the lady. A lady will offer her lips to be kissed only to a lover or a husband, and not to him in company. The French code is a good one: "Give your hand to a gentleman to kiss, your cheek to a friend, but keep your lips for your lover."

Never prescribe any forfeiture that can wound the feelings of any of the company, and "pay" those which may be adjudged to you with cheerful promptness.

DANCING

An evening party is often only another name for a ball. We may have as many and as weighty objections to dancing, as conducted at these fashionable parties, as to the formal dinners and rich and late suppers which are in vogue in the same circles, but this is not the place to discuss the merits of the quadrille or the waltz, but to lay down the etiquette of the occasions on which they are practiced. We condense from the various authorities before us the following code:

- According to the hours now in fashion in our large cities, ten o'clock is quite early enough to present yourself at a dance. You will even then find many coming after you. In the country, you should go earlier.
- Draw on your gloves (white or yellow) in the dressing-room, and do not be for one moment with them off in the dancing-rooms. At supper take them off; nothing is more preposterous than to eat in gloves.
- When you are sure of a place in the dance, you go up to a lady and ask her if she will *do you the honor* to dance with you. If she answers that she is engaged, merely request her to name the earliest dance for which she is not engaged, and when she will do you the honor of dancing with you.

- If a gentleman offers to dance with a lady, she should not refuse, unless for some *particular* and *valid* reason, in which case she can accept the next offer. But if she has no further objection than a temporary dislike or a piece of coquetry, it is a direct insult to him to refuse him and accept the next offer; besides, it shows too marked a preference for the latter.

- When a woman is standing in a quadrille, though not engaged in dancing, a man not acquainted with her partner should not converse with her.

- When an unpracticed dancer makes a mistake, we may apprise him of his error; but it would be very impolite to have the air of giving him a lesson.

- Unless a man has a very graceful figure, and can use it with great elegance, it is better for him to *walk* through the quadrilles [a style of group dancing], or invent some gliding movement for the occasion.

- At the end of the dance, the gentleman re-conducts the lady to her place, bows, and thanks her for the honor that she has conferred. She also bows in silence.

- The master of the house should see that all the ladies dance. He should take notice particularly of those who seem to serve as *drapery* to the walls of the ballroom (or *wallflowers*, as the familiar expression is), and should see that they are invited to dance.

- Ladies who dance much should be very careful not to boast before those who dance but little or not at all, of the great number of dances for which they are engaged in advance. They should also, without being perceived, recommend these less fortunate ladies to gentlemen of their acquaintance.

- For any of the members, either sons or daughters, of the family at whose house the ball is given, to dance frequently or constantly denotes decided ill-breeding; the ladies should not occupy those places in a quadrille which others may wish to fill, and they should, moreover, be at leisure to attend to the rest of the company; and the gentlemen should be entertaining the married women and those who do not dance.

- Never hazard taking part in a quadrille, unless you know how to dance tolerably; for if you are a novice, or but little skilled, you would bring disorder into the midst of pleasure.

- If you accompany your wife to a dance, be careful not to dance with her, except perhaps the first set.

- When that long and anxiously desiderated hour, the hour of supper, has arrived, you hand the lady you attend up or down to the supper-table. You remain with her while she is at the table, seeing that she has all that she desires, and then conduct her back to the dancing-rooms.

- A gentleman attending a lady should invariably dance the first set with her, and may afterward introduce her to a friend for the purpose of dancing.

This code must be understood as applying in full only to fashionable dancing parties in the city, though most of the rules should be adhered to in any place. The good sense of the reader will enable him to modify them to suit any particular occasion.

ANNUAL FESTIVALS

CHRISTMAS

At Christmas, people give parties and make presents. In Europe, and in some portions of the United States, it is the most important festive occasion in the year. Beyond the religious observances of the Catholics, Episcopalians, and some other sects, and the universal custom of making presents to all our relatives and intimate friends, and especially to the children, there is no matter of etiquette peculiar to Christmas that it is necessary for us to note. We have already spoken of presents; and religious ceremonies will find a place in another chapter.

THE NEW YEAR

In New York, and some other cities and towns which have adopted its customs, every gentleman is expected to call on all his lady acquaintances on New Year's Day; and each lady on her part must be prepared properly to do the honors of her house. Refreshments are usually provided in great profusion. The etiquette of these occasions does not differ materially from that of ceremonious morning calls, except that the entire day is devoted to them, and they may be extended beyond the limits of one's ordinary visiting list. The ladies may make their calls on the next day, or any time within the week.

Thanksgiving

This is the great family festival of New England—the season of home gatherings. Sons and daughters, scattered far and wide, then turn instinctively toward the old homestead, and the fireside of their childhood is again made glad by their presence and that of their little ones. Etiquette requires fat turkeys, well roasted, a plenty of pumpkin pies, unbounded hospitality, genuine friendliness, and cheerful and thankful hearts.

Birthdays

Birthdays are sometimes made family festivals at which parties are given, and presents made to the one whose anniversary is celebrated. In France, these occasions are observed with great merry making and many felicitations and gifts.

EXCURSIONS & PICNICS

Picnic excursions into the country are not occasions of ceremony, but call for the exercise of all one's real good nature and good breeding. On leaving the carriage, cars, or steamboat, gentlemen should of course relieve the ladies they attend of the shawls, baskets, etc., with which they may have provided themselves, and give them all necessary assistance in reaching the spot selected for the festivities. It is also their duty and their happiness to accompany them in their rambles, when it is the pleasure of the fair ones to require their attendance, but *not* to be *obtrusive*. They may sometimes wish to be alone.

If a lady chooses to seat herself upon the ground, you are not at liberty to follow her example unless she invites you to be seated. She must not have occasion to think of the possibility of any impropriety on your part. You are her servant, protector, and guard of honor. You will of course give her your hand to assist her in rising.

When the repast is served, you will see that the ladies whose cavalier you have the honor to be, lack nothing. The ladies, social queens though they be, should not forget that every favor or act of courtesy and deference, by whoever shown, demands some acknowledgment on their part—a word, a bow, a smile, or at least a kind look.

WEDDINGS

We copy from one of the numerous manners books before us the following condensed account of the usual ceremonies of a formal wedding. A simpler, less ceremonious, and more private mode of giving legal sanction to an already existing union of hearts would be more to *our* taste; but, as the French proverb has it, *Chacun à son gout* ["to each his own taste"].

For a stylish wedding, the lady requires a bridegroom, two bridesmaids, two groomsmen, and a parson or magistrate, her relatives and whatever friends of both parties they may choose to invite.

A white lace veil is often worn on the head.

For a formal wedding in the evening, a week's notice is requisite. The lady fixes the day. Her mother or nearest female relation invites the guests. The evening hour is eight o'clock; but if the ceremony is private, and the happy couple to start immediately and alone, the ceremony usually takes place in the morning at eleven or twelve o'clock.

If there is an evening party, the refreshments must be as usual on such occasions, with the addition of wedding cake, commonly a pound cake with rich frosting, and a fruit cake.

The dress of the bride is of the purest white; her head is commonly dressed with orange flowers, natural or artificial, and white roses. She wears few ornaments, and none but such as are given her for the occasion. A white lace veil is often worn on the head. White long gloves and white satin slippers complete the costume.

The dress of the bridegroom is simply the full dress of a gentleman, of unusual richness and elegance.

The bridesmaids are dressed also in white, but more simply than the bride.

At the hour appointed for the ceremony, the second brides-maid and groomsman, when there are two, enter the room; then, first bridesmaid and groomsman; and lastly the bride and bridegroom. They enter, the ladies taking the arms of the gentlemen, and take seats appointed, so that the bride is at the right of the bridegroom, and each supported by their respective attendants.

A chair is then placed for the clergyman or magistrate in front of the happy pair. When he comes forward to perform the ceremony, the bridal party rises. The first bridesmaid, at the proper time, removes the glove from the left hand of the bride; or, what seems to us more proper, both bride and bridegroom have their gloves removed at the beginning of the ceremony. In joining hands they take each other's right hand, the bride and groom partially turning toward each other. The wedding ring, of plain fine gold, provided beforehand by the groom, is sometimes given to the clergyman, who presents it. It is placed upon the third finger of the left hand.

> In joining hands they take each other's right hand, the bride and groom partially turning toward each other.

When the ceremony is ended, and the twain are pronounced one flesh, the company present their congratulations —the clergyman first, then the mother, the father of the bride, and the relations; then the company, the groomsmen acting as masters of ceremonies, bringing forward and introducing the ladies, who wish the happy couple joy, happiness, prosperity; but not exactly "many happy returns."

The bridegroom takes an early occasion to thank the clergyman, and to put in his hand, at the same time, nicely enveloped, a piece of gold, according to his ability and generosity. The gentleman who dropped two half-dollars into the minister's hands, as they were held out, in the prayer, was a little confused by the occasion.

According to the *Illustrated Manners Book*, when a dance follows the ceremony and congratulations, the bride dances, first, with the first groomsman, taking the head of the room and the quadrille, and the bridegroom with the first bridesmaid; afterward as they please. The party breaks up early—certainly by twelve o'clock.

The cards of the newly married couple are sent to those only whose acquaintance they wish to continue. No offense should be taken by those whom they may choose to exclude. Send your card, therefore, with the lady's, to all whom you desire to include in the circle of your future acquaintances. The lady's card will have engraved upon it, below her name, "At home, — evening, at — o'clock." They should be sent a week previous to the evening indicated.

FUNERALS

When any member of a family is dead, it is customary to send intelligence of the misfortune to all who have been connected with the deceased in relations of business or friendship. The letters that are sent contain a special invitation to assist at the funeral. Such a letter requires no answer.

At an interment or funeral service, the members of the family are entitled to the first places. They are nearest to the coffin, whether in the procession or in the church. The nearest relations go in a full mourning dress.

We are excused from accompanying the body to the burying-ground, unless the deceased be a relation or an intimate friend. If we go as far as the burying-ground, we should give the first carriage to the relations or most intimate friends of the deceased. We should walk with the head uncovered, silently, and with such a mien as the occasion naturally suggests.

CHAPTER VIII

THE ETIQUETTE OF PLACES

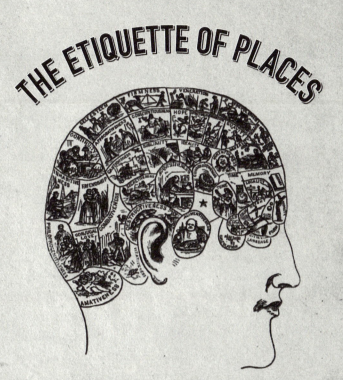

To ladies always yield your seat,
And lift your hat upon the street.

—UNCLE DAN

ON THE STREET

Nowhere has a man or a woman occasion more frequently to exercise the virtue of courtesy than on the street; and in no place is the distinction between the polite and the vulgar more marked. The following are some of the rules of street etiquette:

- Except in a case of necessity, you should not stop a businessman on the street during business hours. He may have appointments, and, in any event, his time is precious. If you must speak with him, walk on in his direction, or if you detain him, state your errand briefly, and politely apologize for the detention.

- Do not allow yourself to be so absentminded or absorbed in your business as not to recognize and salute your acquaintances on the street. You must not make the pressure of your affairs an excuse for rudeness. If you do not intend to stop, on meeting a friend, touch your hat, say "Good-morning," or "I hope you are well," and pass on. If you stop, you may offer a gloved hand, if necessary, without apology. Waiting to draw off a tight glove is awkward.

- In stopping to talk on the street, you should step aside from the human current. If you are compelled to detain a friend, when he is walking with a stranger, apologize to the stranger and release your friend as soon as possible. The stranger will withdraw, in order not to hear your conversation. Never leave a friend suddenly on the street, either to join another or for any other reason, without a brief apology.

- In walking with gentlemen who are your superiors in age or station, give them the place of honor, by taking yourself the outer side of the pavement.

- When you meet a lady with whom you are acquainted, you should lift your hat, as you bow to her; but unless you are intimate friends, it is the lady's duty to give some sign of recognition first, as she might *possibly* choose to "cut" you, and thus place you in a very awkward position; but unless you have forfeited all claims to respect, she certainly *should* not do such a thing.

- As Colonel Henry Lunettes advises, in meeting a gentleman whom you know, walking with a lady with whom you are not acquainted, you are to bow with grave respect to her also. If you are acquainted with both, you bow first to the lady, and then, less profoundly, to the gentleman.

- If your glove be dark colored, or your hand ungloved, do not offer to shake hands with a lady in full dress. If you wish to speak with a lady whom you meet on the street, turn and walk with her; but you should not accompany her far, except at her request, and should always lift your hat and bow upon withdrawing.

- Be careful to avoid intrusion everywhere; and for this reason be very sure that such an addition to their party would be perfectly agreeable before you join a lady and gentleman who may be walking together; otherwise you might find yourself in the position of an "awkward third."

- In walking with ladies on the street, gentlemen will of course treat them with the most scrupulous *politeness*. This requires that you place yourself in that relative position in which you can best shield them from danger or inconvenience. You generally give them the wall side, but circumstances may require you to reverse this position.

- You must offer your arm to a lady with whom you are walking whenever her safety, comfort, or convenience may seem to require such attention on your part. At night, in taking a long walk in the country, or in ascending the steps of a public building, your arm should always be tendered.

> **You must offer your arm to a lady with whom you are walking whenever her safety, comfort, or convenience may seem to require such attention on your part.**

- In walking with ladies or elderly people, a gentleman must not forget to accommodate his speed to theirs. In walking with *any* person you should *keep step* with military precision.

- If a lady with whom you are walking receives the salute of a person who is a stranger to you, you should return it, not for yourself, but for her.

- When a lady whom you accompany wishes to enter a shop, or *store* (if we must use an Americanism to explain a good English word), you should hold the door open and allow her to enter first, if practicable; for you must never pass before a lady anywhere, if you can avoid it, or without an apology.

- If a lady addresses an inquiry to a gentleman on the street, he will lift his hat, or at least touch it respectfully, as he replies. If he cannot give the information required, he will express his regrets.

> You should dress well—neatly and in good taste, and in material adapted to the season.

- "When tripping over the pavement," Madame Celnart says, "a lady should gracefully raise her dress a little above her ankle. With her right hand she should hold together the folds of her gown and draw them toward the right side. To raise the dress on both sides, and with both hands, is vulgar. This ungraceful practice can be tolerated only for a moment, when the mud is very deep." This was written in Paris, and not in New York.

- American ladies dress too richly and elaborately for the street. You should dress well—neatly and in good taste, and in material adapted to the season; but the full costume, suitable to the carriage or the drawing-room, is entirely out of place in a shopping excursion, and does not indicate a refined taste; in other words, it looks *snobbish*.

- The outdoor costume of ladies is not complete without a shawl or a mantle. Shawls are difficult to wear gracefully, and few American ladies wear them well. You should not drag a shawl tight to your shoulders, and stick out your elbows, but fold it loosely and gracefully, so that it may fully envelop the figure.

SHOPPING

Madame Celnart has the following hints to the ladies on this important subject. Having enjoined the most patient and forbearing courtesy on the part of the shopkeeper, she proceeds:

> "Every civility ought to be reciprocal, or nearly so. If the officious politeness of the shopkeeper does not require an equal return, he has at least a claim to civil treatment; and, finally, if this politeness proceed from interest, is this a reason why purchasers should add to the unpleasantness of his profession, and disregard violating the laws of politeness? Many very respectable people allow themselves so many

infractions in this particular, that I think it my
duty to dwell upon it.

"You should never say, *I want such a thing*, but
Show me, if you please, that article, or use some
other polite form of address. If they do not show
you at first the articles you desire, and you are
obliged to examine a great number, apologize
to the shopkeeper for the trouble you give him.
If after all you cannot suit yourself, renew your
apologies when you go away.

"If you make small purchases, say, *I am sorry for
having troubled you for so trifling a thing*. If you
spend a considerable time in the selection of
articles, apologize to the shopkeeper who waits
for you to decide.

"If the price seems to you too high, and the
shop has not fixed prices, ask an abatement in
brief and civil terms, and without ever appear-
ing to suspect the good faith of the shopkeeper.
If he does not yield, do not enter into a con-
test with him, but go away, after telling him
politely that you think you can obtain the article
cheaper elsewhere, but if not, that you will give
him the preference."

AT CHURCH

If you go to church, be on time, that you may not interrupt the congregation by entering after the services have commenced. The celebrated Mrs. Hester Chapone, an English writer, said that it was a part of her religion not to disturb the religion of others. We may all adopt with profit that article of her creed.

Always remove your hat on entering a church. If you attend ladies, you open the door of the slip for them, allowing them to enter first.

Your demeanor should of course be such as becomes the place and occasion. If you are so unfortunate as to have no religious feelings yourself, you must respect those of others.

It is the custom in some places for gentlemen who may be already in a slip or pew to deploy into the aisle, on the arrival of a lady who may desire admittance, allow her to enter, and then resume their seats. This is a very awkward and annoying maneuver.

You should pay due respect to the observances of the church you attend. If you have conscientious scruples against kneeling in an Episcopal or Catholic church, you should be a little more conscientious, and stay away.

Good manners do not require young gentlemen to stand about the door of a church to see the ladies come out; and the ladies will excuse the omission of this mark of admiration.

AT PLACES OF AMUSEMENT

Gentlemen who attend ladies to the opera, to concerts, to lectures, etc., should endeavor to go early in order to secure good seats, unless, indeed, they have been previously secured, and to avoid the disagreeable crowd which they are liable to encounter if they go a little later.

Gentlemen *should* take off their hats on entering *any* public room (or dwelling either). They will, of course, do so if attending ladies, on showing them their seats. Having taken your seats, remain quietly in them, and avoid, unless absolute necessity requires it, incommoding others by crowding out and in before them. If obliged to do this, politely apologize for the trouble you cause them.

To talk during the performance is an act of rudeness and injustice. You thus proclaim your own ill-breeding and invade the rights of others, who have paid for the privilege of hearing the performers, and not for listening to you.

If you are in attendance upon a lady at any opera, concert, or lecture, you should retain your seat at her side; but if you have no lady with you, and have taken a desirable seat, you should, if need be, cheerfully relinquish it in favor of a lady, for one less eligible.

Be careful to secure your *libretto* or opera book, concert bill or program, before taking your seat.

To the opera, ladies should wear opera hoods, which are to be taken off on entering. In this country, custom *permits* the wearing of bonnets; but as they are (in our opinion) neither comfortable nor beautiful, we advise the ladies to dispense with their use whenever they can.

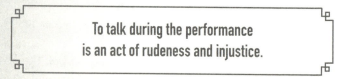

To talk during the performance is an act of rudeness and injustice.

Gloves should be worn by ladies in church, and in places of public amusement. Do not take them off to shake hands. Great care should be taken that they are well made and fit neatly.

IN A PICTURE GALLERY

A gallery of paintings or sculpture is a temple of art, and he is little better than a barbarian who can enter it without a feeling of reverence for the presiding divinity of the place. Loud talking, laughing, pushing before others who are examining a picture or statue, moving seats noisily, or any rude or discourteous conduct, seems like profanation in such a place. Avoid them by all means, we entreat you; and though you wear your hat everywhere else, reverently remove it here. . . .

TRAVELING

Under no circumstances is courtesy more urgently demanded, or rudeness more frequently displayed, than in traveling. The infelicities and vexations that so often attend a journey seem to call out all the latent selfishness of one's nature; and the commonest observances of politeness are, we are sorry to say, sometimes neglected. In the scramble for tickets, for seats, for state-rooms, or for places at a public table, good manners are too frequently elbowed aside and trampled under foot. Even our national deference for women is occasionally lost sight of in our headlong rush for the railway cars or the steamer.

To avoid the scramble we have alluded to, purchase tickets and secure state-rooms in advance, if practicable, especially if you are accompanied by ladies, and, in any event, *be in good time*.

In the cars or stagecoach never allow considerations of personal comfort or convenience to cause you to disregard for a moment the rights of your fellow-travelers, or forget the respectful courtesy due to women. The pleasantest or most comfortable seats belong to the ladies, and no gentleman will refuse to resign such seats to them with a cheerful politeness. In a stagecoach you give them the back seat, unless they prefer another, and take an outside seat yourself, if their convenience requires it. But a word to *Americans* will be enough on this point.

And what do good manners require of the ladies? That which is but a little thing to the bestower, but of priceless value to the receiver—*thanks*—a smile—a grateful look at least. Is this too much?

Mr. Arbiter, whom we find quoted in a newspaper, has some rather severe strictures on the conduct of American ladies. He says:

> "We boast of our politeness as a nation, and point out to foreigners, with pride, the alacrity with which Americans make way for women in all public places. Some love to call this chivalry. It is certainly an amiable trait of character, though frequently carried to an absurd extent. But what the men possess in this form of politeness the women appear to have lost. They never think of acknowledging, in any way, the kindness of the gentleman who gives up his seat, but settle themselves triumphantly in their new places, as if they were entitled to them by divine right."

We are compelled to admit that there is at least an appearance of truth in this charge. We have had constant opportunities to observe the behavior of ladies in omnibuses and on board the crowded ferryboats that ply between some of our large cities and their suburbs. We have, of course (as what gentleman has not?), relinquished our seats hundreds of times to ladies. *For the occasional bow or smile of acknowledgment, or pleasant "Thank you," which we have received in return, we have almost invariably been indebted to some fair foreigner.*

We believe that American ladies are as polite *at heart* as those of any other nation, but *they do not say it.*

The fair readers of our little book will, we are sure, excuse us for these hints, since they are dictated by the truest and most reverent love for their sex, and a sincere desire to serve them.

If in traveling you are thrown into the company of an invalid, or an aged person, or a woman with children and without a male protector, feelings of humanity, as well as sentiments of politeness, will dictate such kind attentions as, without being obtrusive, you can find occasion to bestow.

You have no right to keep a window open for your accommodation, if the current of air thus produced annoy or endanger the health of another. There are a sufficient number of discomforts in traveling, at best, and it should be the aim of each passenger to lessen them as much as possible, and to cheerfully bear his own part. Life is a journey, and we are all fellow-travelers.

If in riding in an omnibus, or crossing a ferry with a friend, he wishes to pay for you, never insist on paying for yourself or for both. If he is before you, let the matter pass without remark, and return the compliment on another occasion.

CHAPTER IX

LOVE AND COURTSHIP

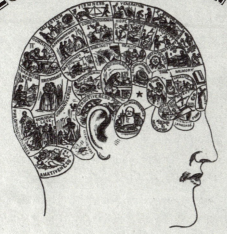

Learn to win a lady's faith
Nobly, as the thing is high;
Bravely, as for life and death,
With a loyal gravity.
Lead her from the festive boards;
Point her to the starry skies;
Guard her by your truthful words
Pure from courtship's flatteries.

—Elizabeth Barrett Browning

A HINT OR TWO

To treat the subject of love and courtship in all its bearings would require a volume. It is with the etiquette of the tender passion that we have to do here. A few preliminary hints, however, will not be deemed out of place.

Boys often fall in love (and girls too, we believe) at a very tender age. Some charming cousin, or a classmate of his sister, in the village school, weaves silken meshes around the throbbing heart of the young man in his teens. This is well. He is made better and happier by his boyish loves—for he generally has a succession of them, but they are seldom permanent. They are only beautiful foreshadowings of the deeper and more earnest love of manhood, which is to bind him to his *other self* with ties which only death can sever. Read Donald Grant Mitchell's *Dream Life, a Fable of the Seasons*.

> **Boys often fall in love (and girls too, we believe) at a very tender age.**

Before a young man has reached the proper age to marry—say twenty-five, as an average—he ought to have acquired such a knowledge of himself, physically and mentally considered, and of the principles which ought to decide the choice of matrimonial partners and govern the relations of the sexes, as will enable him to set up a proper standard of female excellence, and to determine what qualities, physical and mental, should characterize the woman who is to be the angel of his home and the mother of his children. With this knowledge he is prepared to go into society and choose his mate, following trustingly the attractions of his soul. Love is an affair of the heart, but the head should be its privy counselor.

> **Love is an affair of the heart,
> but the head should be its privy counselor.**

Do not make up your mind to wait till you have acquired a fortune before you marry. You should not, however, assume the responsibilities of a family without a reasonable prospect of being able to maintain one. If you are established in business, or have an adequate income for the immediate requirements of the new relation, you may safely trust your own energy and self-reliance for the rest.

Women reach maturity earlier than men, and may marry earlier—say (as an average age), at twenty. The injunction, "Know thyself," applies with as much emphasis to a woman as to a man. Her perceptions are keener than ours, and her sensibilities finer, and she may trust more to *instinct*, but she should add to these natural qualifications a thorough knowledge of her own physical and mental constitution, and of whatever relates to the requirements of her destiny as wife and mother. The importance of sound *health* and *a perfect development* cannot be overrated. *Without these you are* NEVER *fit to marry.*

Having satisfied yourself that you really love a woman—be careful, as you value your future happiness and hers, not to make a *mistake* in this matter—you will find occasion to manifest, in a thousand ways, your preference, by means of those tender but delicate and deferential attentions which love always prompts. "Let the heart speak." The heart you address will understand its language. Be earnest, sincere, self-loyal, and manly in this matter above all others. Let there be no nauseous flattery and no sickly sentimentality. Leave the former to fops and the latter to beardless schoolboys.

> The heart you address will understand its language. Be earnest, sincere, self-loyal, and manly in this matter above all others.

Though women do not "propose"—that is, as a general rule—they "make love" to the men nonetheless; and it is right. The divine attraction is mutual, and should have its proper expression on both sides. If you are attracted toward a man who seems to you an embodiment of all that is noble and manly, you do injustice both to him and yourself if you do not, in some way entirely consistent with maiden modesty, allow him to *see* and *feel* that he pleases you. But *you* do not need our instructions, and we will only hint, in conclusion, that forwardness, flirting, and a too *obtrusive* manifestation of preference are *not* agreeable to men of sense. As a man should be *manly*, so should a woman be *womanly* in her love.

OBSERVANCES

Particular Attentions

Avoid even the slightest appearance of *trifling* with the feelings of a woman. A female coquette is bad enough. A male coquette ought to be banished from society. Let there be a clearly perceived, if not an easily defined, distinction between the attentions of common courtesy or of friendship and those of love. All misunderstanding on this point can and must be avoided.

The particular attentions you pay to the object of your devotion should not make you rude or uncivil to other women. Every woman is *her* sister, and should be treated with becoming respect and attention. Your special attentions to her in society should not be such as to make her or you the subject of ridicule. Make no public exhibition of your endearments.

> A female coquette is bad enough.
> A male coquette ought to be banished from society.

Presents

If you [give] presents, let them be selected with good taste, and of such cost as is fully warranted by your means. Your mistress will not love you better for any extravagance in this matter. The value of a gift is not to be estimated in dollars and cents. A lady of good sense and delicacy will discourage in her lover all needless expenditure in ministering to her gratification, or in proof of his devotion.

CONFIDANTS

Lovers usually feel a certain need of confidants in their affairs of the heart. In general, they should be of the opposite sex. A young man may with profit open his heart to his mother, an elder sister, or a female friend considerably older than himself. The young lady may with equal advantage make a brother, an uncle, or some good middle-aged married man the repository of her love secrets, her hopes, and her fears.

DECLARATIONS

We shall make no attempt to prescribe a form for "popping the question." Each must do it in his own way; but let it be clearly understood and admit no evasion. A single word—yes, less than that, on the lady's part, will suffice to answer it. If the carefully studied phrases, which you have repeated so many times and so fluently to yourself, will persist in sticking in your throat and choking you, put them correctly and neatly on a sheet of the finest white note paper, enclosed in a fine but plain white envelope, seal it handsomely with *wax*, address and direct it carefully, and find some way to convey it to her hand. The lady's answer should be frank and unequivocal, revealing briefly and modestly her real feelings and consequent decision.

Asking "Pa"

Asking the consent of parents or guardians is, in this country, where women claim a right to choose for themselves, a mere form, and may often be dispensed with. The lady's wishes, however, should be complied with in this as in all other matters.

And if consent is refused? This will rarely happen. If it does, there is a remedy, and we should have a poor opinion of the love or the spirit of the woman who would hesitate to apply it. If she is of age, she has a legal as well as a moral right to bestow her love and her hand upon whom she pleases. If she does not love you well enough to do this, *at any sacrifice*, you should consider the refusal of her friends a very fortunate occurrence. If she is not of age, the legal aspect of the affair may be different, but, at worst, she can wait until her majority puts her in possession of all her rights.

Refusals

If a lady finds it necessary to say "no" to a proposal, she should do it in the kindest and most considerate manner, so as not to inflict unnecessary pain; but her answer should be definite and decisive, and the gentleman should at once withdraw his suit. If ladies will say "no" when they mean "yes," to a sincere and earnest suitor, they must suffer the consequences.

ENGAGEMENT

The "engaged" need not take particular pains to proclaim the nature of the relation in which they stand to each other, neither should they attempt or desire to conceal it. Their intercourse with each other should be frank and confiding, but prudent, and their conduct in reference to other persons of the opposite sex, such as will not give occasion for a single pang of jealousy.

Of the "getting ready," which follows the engagement, on the part of the lady, our fair readers know a great deal more than we could tell them.

BREAKING OFF

Engagements made in accordance with the simple and brief directions contained in the first section of this chapter will seldom be broken off. If such a painful *necessity* occurs, let it be met with firmness, but with delicacy. If you have made a *mistake*, it is infinitely better to correct it at the last moment than not at all. A *marriage* is not so easily "broken off."

> If you have made a *mistake*, it is infinitely better to correct it at the last moment than not at all.

On breaking off an engagement, all letters, presents, etc., should be returned, and both parties should consider themselves pledged to the most honorable and delicate conduct in reference to the whole matter, and to the private affairs of each other, a knowledge of which their former relation may have put into their possession.

MARRIAGE

It devolves upon the lady to fix the day. She will hardly disregard the stereotyped request of the impatient lover to make it an "early" one; but she knows best how soon the never-to-be-neglected "preparations" can be made. For the wedding ceremonies see Chapter VII. A few hints to husbands and wives may be found in Chapter V.

Chapter X

THE ETIQUETTE OF POLITICS

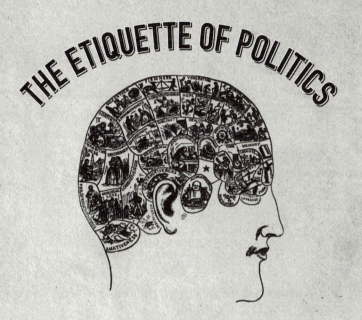

The object of a meeting for deliberation is, of course, to obtain a free expression of opinion and a fair decision of the questions discussed. Without rules of order this object would, in most cases, be utterly defeated; for there would be no uniformity in the modes of proceeding, no restraint upon indecorous or disorderly conduct, no protection to the rights and privileges of members, no guarantee against the caprices and usurpations of the presiding officer, no safeguard against tyrannical majorities, nor any suitable regard to the rights of the minority.

—James Napoleon McElligott

COURTESY IN DEBATE

The fundamental principles of courtesy, so strenuously insisted upon throughout this work, must be rigorously observed in the debating society, lyceum, legislative assembly, and wherever questions are publicly debated. In fact, we have not yet discovered *any* occasion on which a gentleman is justified in being anything less than—a gentleman.

In a paragraph appended to the constitution and by-laws of a New York debating club, members are enjoined to:

- Treat each other with delicacy and respect
- Conduct all discussions with candor, moderation, and open generosity
- Avoid all personal allusions and sarcastic language calculated to wound the feelings of a brother
- Cherish concord and good fellowship

The spirit of this injunction should pervade the heart of every man who attempts to take part in the proceedings of any deliberative assembly.

RULES OF ORDER

Motions

A deliberative body being duly organized, motions are in order. The party moving a resolution, or making a motion in its simplest form, introduces it either with or without remarks, by saying: "Mr. President, I beg leave to offer the following resolution," or "I move that," etc. A motion is not debatable till seconded. The member seconding simply says: "I second that motion." The resolution or motion is then stated by the chairman, and is open for debate.

Speaking

A member wishing to speak on a question, resolution, or motion must rise in his place and respectfully address his remarks to the chairman or president, *confining himself to the question, and avoiding personality*. Should more than one member rise at the same time, the chairman must decide which is entitled to the floor.

No member must speak more than once till every member wishing to speak shall have spoken. In debating societies (and it is for their benefit that we make this abstract) it is necessary to define not only how many times but also how long at each time a member may speak on a question.

Submitting a Question

When the debate or deliberation upon a subject appears to be at a close, the presiding officer simply asks, "Is the society [assembly, or whatever the body may be] ready for the question?" or, "Are you ready for the question?" If no one signifies a desire further to discuss or consider the subject, he then submits the question in due form.

Voting

The voting is generally by "ayes and noes," and the answers on both sides being duly given, the presiding officer announces the result, saying, "The ayes have it," or, "The noes have it," according as he finds one side or the other in the majority. If there is a doubt in his mind which side has the larger number, he says, "The ayes *appear* to have it," or, "The noes *appear* to have it," as the case may be. If there is no dissent, he adds, "The ayes *have* it," or, "The noes *have* it."

But should the president be unable to decide, or if his decision is questioned, and a division of the house be called for, it is his duty immediately to divide or arrange the assembly as to allow the votes on each side to be accurately counted; and if the members are equally divided, the president must give the casting vote.

It is the duty of every member to vote.

It is the duty of every member to vote; but in some deliberative bodies a member may be excused at his own request. Sometimes it is deemed advisable to record the names of members in connection with the votes they give, in which case the roll is called by the secretary, and each answers "yes" or "no," which is noted or marked opposite his name.

A Quorum

A quorum is such a number of members as may be required, by rule or statute, to be present at a meeting in order to render its transactions valid or legal.

The Democratic Principle

All questions, unless their decision is otherwise fixed by law, are determined by a majority of votes.

Privileged Questions

There are certain motions that are allowed to supersede a question already under debate. These are called privileged questions. The following are the usually recognized privileged questions:

1. *Adjournment.*—A motion to adjourn is always in order, and takes precedence of all others; but it must not be entertained while a member is speaking, unless he give way for that purpose, nor while a vote is in progress. It is not debatable, and cannot be amended.

2. *To Lie on the Table.*—A motion to lay a subject on the table—that is, to set it aside till it is the pleasure of the body to resume its consideration—generally takes precedence of all others, except the motion to adjourn. It can neither be debated nor amended.

3. *The Previous Question.*—The intention of the previous question is to arrest discussion and test at once the sense of the meeting. Its form is, "Shall the main question now be put?" It is not debatable, and cannot be amended. An affirmative decision precludes all further debate on the main question. The effect of a negative decision, *unless otherwise determined by a special rule*, is to leave the main question and all amendments just as it found them.

4. *Postponement.*—A motion to postpone the consideration of a question indefinitely, which is equivalent to setting it aside altogether, may be amended by inserting a certain day. It is not debatable.

5. *Commitment.*—A motion to commit is made when a question, otherwise admissible, is presented in an objectionable or inconvenient form. If there be no standing committee to which it can be properly submitted, a select committee may be raised for the purpose. It may be amended.

6. *Amendment.*—The legitimate use of a motion to amend is to correct or improve the original motion or resolution; but a motion properly before an assembly may be altered in *any* way; even so as to turn it entirely from its original purpose, unless some rule or law shall exist to prevent this subversion. An amendment may be amended, but here the process must cease. An amendment must of course be put to vote before the original question. A motion to amend holds the same rank as the previous question and indefinite postponement, and that which is moved first must be put first. It may be

superseded, however, by a motion to postpone to a certain day, or a motion to commit.

7. *Orders of the Day.*—Subjects appointed for a specified time are called orders of the day, and a motion for them takes precedence of all other business, except a motion to adjourn, or a question of privilege.

8. *Questions of Privilege.*—These are questions which involve the rights and privileges of individual members, or of the society or assembly collectively. They take precedence over all other propositions, except a motion to adjourn.

9. *Questions of Order.*—In case of any breach of the rules of the society or body, any member may rise to the point of order, and insist upon its due enforcement; but in case of a difference of opinion whether a rule has been violated or not, the question must be determined before the application of the rule can be insisted upon. Such a question is usually decided upon by the presiding officer, without debate; but any member may appeal from his decision, and demand a vote of the house on the matter. A question of order is debatable, and the presiding officer, contrary to rule in other cases, may participate in the discussion.

10. *Reading of Papers.*—When papers or documents of any kind are laid before a deliberative assembly, every member has a right to have them read before he can be required to vote upon them. They are generally read by the secretary, on the reading being called for, without the formality of a vote.

11. *Withdrawal of a Motion.*—Unless there is a rule to that effect, a motion once before the assembly cannot be withdrawn without a vote of the house, on a motion to allow its withdrawal.

12. *The Suspension of Rules.*—When anything is proposed which is forbidden by a special rule, it must be preceded by a motion for the suspension of the rule, which, if there is no standing rule to the contrary, may be carried by a majority of votes; but most deliberative bodies have an established rule on this subject, requiring a fixed proportion of the votes—usually two-thirds.

13. *The Motion to Reconsider.*—The intention of this is to enable an assembly to revise a decision found to be erroneous. The time within which a motion to reconsider may be entertained is generally fixed by a special rule; and the general rule is, that it must emanate from some member who voted with the majority. In Congress, a motion to reconsider takes precedence of all other motions, except the motion to adjourn.

ORDER OF BUSINESS

In all permanently organized bodies there should be an order of business, established by a special rule or by-law; but where no such rule or law exists, the president, unless otherwise directed by a vote of the assembly, arranges the business in such order as he may think most desirable.

The following is the order of business of the New York Debating Club, referred to in a previous section. It may be easily so modified as to be suitable for any similar society:

1. Call to order.
2. Calling the roll.
3. Reading the minutes of previous meeting.
4. Propositions for membership.
5. Reports of special committee.
6. Balloting for candidates.
7. Reports of standing committee.
8. Secretary's report.
9. Treasurer's report.
10. Reading for the evening.
11. Recitations for the evening.
12. Candidates initiated.
13. Unfinished business.
14. Debate.
15. New business.
16. Adjournment.

ORDER OF DEBATE

The following rules of order have been mainly condensed from that excellent work, *The American Debater*, by James N. McElligott, LL.D., to which the reader is referred for a complete exposition of the whole subject of debating.

1. A member having got the floor is entitled to be heard to the end, or till the time fixed by rule has expired; and all interruptions, except a call to order, are not only out of order, but rude in the extreme.

2. A member who temporarily yields the floor to another is generally permitted to resume as soon as the interruption ceases, but he cannot claim to do so as a right.

3. It is neither in order nor in good taste to designate members by name in debate, and they must in no case be directly addressed. Such forms as, "The gentleman who has just taken his seat," or, "The member on the other side of the house," etc., may be made use of to designate persons.

4. Every speaker is bound to confine himself to the question. This rule is, however, very liberally interpreted in most deliberative assemblies.

5. Every speaker is bound to avoid personalities, and to exercise in all respects a courteous and gentlemanly deportment. Principles and measures are to be discussed, and not the motives or character of those who advocate them.

CHAPTER XI

MISCELLANEOUS MATTERS

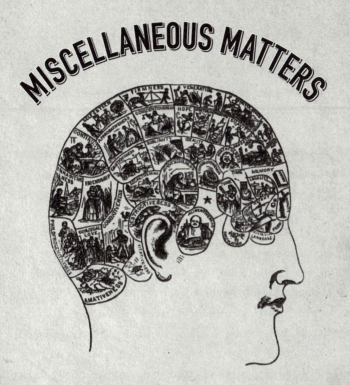

These, some will say, are little things. It is true, they are little but it is equally clear that they are necessary things.

—Lord Chesterfield

REPUBLICAN DISTINCTIONS

We have defined equality in another place. We fully accept the doctrine as there set forth. We have no respect for mere conventional and arbitrary distinctions. Hereditary titles command no deference from us. Lords and dukes are entitled to no respect simply because they are lords and dukes. If they are really *noble men*, we honor them accordingly. Their titles are mere social fictions. . . .

The error committed by our professedly republican communities consists, not in the recognition of classes and grades of rank, but in placing them, as they too often do, on artificial and not on natural grounds. . . .

We have in our country a class of toad-eaters who delight in paying the most obsequious homage to fictitious rank of every kind. A vulgar millionaire of the Fifth Avenue, and a foreign adventurer with a meaningless title, are equally objects of their misplaced deference. Losing sight of their own manhood and self-respect, they descend to the most degrading sycophancy. We have little hope of benefiting them. They are "joined to their idols; let them alone."

But a much larger class of our people is inclined to go to the opposite extreme, and ignore veneration, in its human aspect, altogether. They have no reverence for anybody or anything. This class of people will read our book, and, we trust, profit by its well-meant hints. We respect them, though we cannot always commend their manners. They have independence and manliness, but fail to accord due respect to the manhood of others. It is for their special benefit that we leave touched with considerable emphasis on the deference due to age and *genuine* rank, from whatever source derived.

> [Some people] have independence and manliness, but fail to accord due respect to the manhood of others.

For example, perhaps your townsman, Mr. Dollarmark, has no claim on you for any special token of respect, simply because he inherited half a million, which has grown in his hands to a million and a half, while you cannot count half a thousand, or because he lives in his own palatial mansion, and you in a hired cottage; but your neighbor, Mr. Anvil, who, setting out in life, like yourself, without a penny, has amassed a little fortune by his own unaided exertions, and secured a high social position by his manliness, integrity, and good breeding, is entitled to a certain deference on your part—a recognition of his merits and his superiority.

It is not for birth, or wealth, or occupation, or any other accidental circumstance, that we ask reverence, but for *inherent nobility wrought out in life*. This is what should give men rank and titles in a republic.

CITY & COUNTRY

The words *civil* and *civilized* are derived from the Latin *civitas* (Ital., *città*), a city; and *polite*, from the Greek πολις (*polis*), a city; because cities are the first to become civilized, or *civil*, and polite, or *polished* (Latin, *polire*). They are still, as a general rule, the home of the most highly cultivated people, as well as of the rudest and most degraded, and unquestioned arbiters of fashion and social observances. For this reason the rules of etiquette laid down in this and all other works on the subject of manners are calculated, as the astronomers say, for the meridian of the city.

The observances of the country are borrowed from the city, and modified to suit the social condition and wants of the different localities. This must always be borne in mind, and your behavior regulated accordingly. The white or pale yellow gloves, which you must wear during the whole evening at a fashionable evening party in the city, under pain of being set down as unbearably vulgar, would be very absurd appendages at a social gathering at a farmhouse in the country. None but a *snob* would wear them at such a place. So with other things.

IMPORTED MANNERS

N. P. Willis, in the *Home Journal*, says, "We should be glad to see a distinctly American school of good manners, in which all useless etiquette were thrown aside, but every politeness adopted or invented which could promote sensible and easy exchanges of goodwill and sociability. Good sense and consideration for others should be the basis of every usage of polite life that is worth regarding. Indeed, we have long thought that our country was old enough to adopt measures and etiquettes of its own, based, like all other politeness, upon benevolence and common sense. To get rid of imported etiquette is the first thing to do for American politeness."

This is an important truth well stated. We have had enough of mere imported conventionalism in manners. Our usages should not be English or French usages, further than English and French usages are founded on universal principles. Politeness is the same everywhere and always, but the forms of etiquette must change with times and places; for an observance that may be proper and useful in London or Paris may be abundantly absurd in New York.

FICTITIOUS TITLES

In answer to a correspondent who inquires whether an American citizen should address a European nobleman by his title, *Life Illustrated* says:

> "We answer, unhesitatingly, no. Most of the European titles are purely fictitious, as well as ridiculous. The Duke of Northumberland, for example, has nothing in particular to do with Northumberland, nor does he exercise dukeship (or leadership) over anything except his private estate. The title is a perfect absurdity; it means nothing whatever; it is a mere nickname; and Mr. Percy is a fool for permitting himself to be addressed as 'My Lord Duke,' and 'Your Grace.'
>
> "Indeed, even in England, gentlemen use those titles very sparingly, and servants alone habitually employ then. American citizens who are thrown, in their travels, or in their intercourse with society, into communication with persons bearing titles, may treat them with all due respect without Gracing or My-Lording them. In our opinion, they should do so. And we have faith enough in the good sense of the English people to believe that the next generation, or the

next but one, will see a general abandonment of fictitious titles by the voluntary action of the very people who hold them.

"At the same time, we are inclined to think that the bestowment of real titles—titles which mean something, titles given in recognition of distinguished worth and eminent services, titles not hereditary—will be one of the most cherished prerogatives of the enlightened states of the good time coming. The first step, however, must be the total abolition of all titles which are fictitious and hereditary."

A MIRROR FOR CERTAIN MEN

The following rather broad hints to certain bipeds who *ought* to be gentlemen were clipped from some newspaper. We are sorry we do not know to whom to credit the article:

"Who can tell why women are expected, on pain of censure and avoidance, to conform to a high standard of behavior, while men are indulged in another a great deal lower? We never could fully understand why men should be tolerated in the chewing of tobacco, in smoking, and in spitting everywhere almost, and at all times, whereas a woman cannot do any of these things without exciting aversion and disgust.

"Why ought a man to be allowedly so self-indulgent, putting his limbs and person in all manner of attitudes, however uncouth and distasteful, merely because such vulgarities yield him temporary eases, while a woman is always required to preserve an attitude, if not of positive grace, at least of decency and propriety, from which if she departs, though but for an instant, she forfeits respect, and is instantly branded as a low creature!

"Can anyone say why a man when he has the toothache, or is called to suffer in any other way, should be permitted, as a matter of course, to groan and bellow, and vent his feelings very much in the style of an animal not endowed with reason, while a woman similarly suffering must bear it in silence and decorum? Why should men, as a class, habitually, and as a matter of right, boldly wear the coarsest qualities of human nature on the outside, and swear and fight, and beastify themselves, so that they are obliged to be put into separate pens in the cars on railroads, and at the dépôts, while women must appear with an agreeable countenance, if not in smiles, even when the head, or perhaps the heart, aches, and are expected to permit nothing ill-tempered, disagreeable, or even unhappy to appear outwardly, but to keep all these concealed in their own bosoms to suffer as they may, lest they might otherwise lessen the cheerfulness of others?

"These are a few suggestions only among many we would hint to the stronger and more exciting sex to be reflected on for the improvement of their tastes and manners. In the mirror thus held up before them, they cannot avoid observing the very different standards by which the behavior of the two sexes is constantly regulated. If any reason can be assigned why one should always be a lady, and the other hardly ever a gentleman, we hope it will be done."

WASHINGTON'S CODE OF MANNERS

- Every action ought to be with some sign of respect to those present.
- Be no flatterer; neither play with anyone who delights not to be played with.
- Read no paper or book in company.
- Come not near the papers or books of another when he is writing.
- Let your countenance be cheerful; but in serious matters be grave.
- Let your discourse with others, on matters of business, be short.
- It is good manners to let others speak first.
- When a man does all he can, do not blame him, though he succeeds not well.
- Take admonitions thankfully.
- Be not too hasty to receive lying reports to the injury of another.
- Let your dress be modest, and consult your condition.
- *Play not the peacock by looking vainly at yourself.*
- It is better to be alone than in bad company.
- Let your conversation be without malice or envy.
- Urge not your friend to discover a secret.
- Break not a jest where none take pleasure in mirth.

- Gaze not on the blemishes of others.
- When another speaks, be attentive.

MARKED PASSAGES

On turning over the leaves of the various works on etiquette which we have had occasion to consult in the preparation of this little manual, we have marked with our pencil a large number of passages which seemed to us to embody important facts or thoughts, with the hope of being able to weave them into our work, each in its appropriate place. Some of them we have made use of according to our original intention; a few others not elsewhere used, we purpose to throw together here without any attempt at classification.

Our Social Uniform

The universal partiality of our countrymen for *black*, as the color of dress clothes, at least, is frequently remarked upon by foreigners. Among the best dressed men on the Continent, as well as in England, black, though not confined to the clergy, is in much less general use than here. They adopt the darker shades of blue, brown, and green, and for undress almost as great diversity of colors as of fabrics.

Hints to the Ladies Re: Décor

Don't make your rooms gloomy. Furnish them for light and let them have it. Daylight is very cheap, and candle or gas light you need not use often. If your rooms are dark, all the effect of furniture, pictures, walls, and carpets is lost.

> Furnish [your rooms] for light and let them have it.

If you have beautiful things, make them useful. The fashion of having a nice parlor, and then shutting it up all but three or four days in the year, when you have company; spending your own life in a mean room, shabbily furnished, or an unhealthy basement, to save your things, is the meanest possible economy. Go a little further—shut up your house, and live in a pig-pen! The use of nice and beautiful things is to act upon your spirit—to educate you and make you beautiful.

Don't put your cards around the [mirror], unless in your private boudoir. If you wish to display them, keep them in a suitable basket or vase on the mantle or center-table.

An Obliging Disposition

Polite persons are necessarily obliging. A smile is always on their lips, an earnestness in their countenance, when we ask a favor of them. They know that to render a service with a bad grace is in reality not to render it at all. If they are obliged to refuse a favor, they do it with mildness and delicacy; they express such feeling regret that they still inspire us with gratitude; in short, their conduct appears so perfectly natural that it really seems that the opportunity which is offered them of obliging us, is obliging themselves; and they refuse all our thanks, without affectation or effort.

Securing a Home

Let me, as a somewhat scrutinizing observer of the varying phases of social life, in our own country especially, enter my earnest protest against the practice so commonly adopted by newly married persons, of *boarding*, in place of at once establishing for themselves the distinctive and ennobling prerogatives of HOME. Language and time would alike fail me in an endeavor to set forth the manifold evils inevitably growing out of this fashionable system.

Take the advice of an old man, who has tested theories by prolonged experience, and at once establish your Penates [Roman gods of the household] within four walls, and under a roof that will, at times, exclude all who are not properly denizens of your household, upon assuming the rights and obligations of married life. Do not be deterred from this step by the conviction that you cannot shrine your home deities upon pedestals of marble. *Cover their bases with flowers—* God's free gift to all—and the plainest support will suffice for them if it be but *firm*.

Taste vs. Fashion

A lady should never, on account of economy, wear either what she deems an ugly or an ungraceful garment; such garments never put her at her ease, and are neglected and cast aside long before they have done her their true service. We are careful only of those things that suit us, and which we believe adorn us, and the mere fact of believing that we look well goes a great way toward making us do so.

Fashion should be sacrificed to taste, or, at best, followed at a distance; it does not do to be *entirely out*, nor *completely in*, what is called "fashion," many things being embraced under that term which are frivolous, unmeaning, and sometimes meretricious.

SPECIAL CLAIMS

There are persons to whom a lady or gentleman should be especially polite: all elderly persons, the unattractive, the poor, and those whose dependent positions may cause them to fear neglect. The gentleman who offers his arm or gives his time to an old lady, or asks a very plain one to dance, or attends one who is poorly dressed, never loses in others' estimation or his own.

PROPRIETY OF DEPORTMENT

Propriety of deportment is the valuable result of a knowledge of one's self, and of respect for the rights of others; it is a feeling of the sacrifices which are imposed on self-esteem by our social relations; it is, in short, a sacred requirement of harmony and affection.

FALSE PRIDE

False pride and false dignity are very mean qualities. A true gentleman will do anything proper for him to do. He can soil his hands or use his muscles when there is occasion. The truest gentleman is more likely to carry home a market-basket, or a parcel, or to wheel a barrow through Broadway, than many a conceited little snob of a shop-boy.

THE AWKWARDNESS OF BEING "DRESSED"

When dressed for company, strive to appear as easy and natural as if you were in [casual dress]. Nothing is more distressing to a sensitive person, or more ridiculous to one gifted with an *esprit moquer* [a disposition to "make fun"], than to see a lady laboring under the consciousness of a fine gown; or a gentleman who is stiff, awkward, and ungainly in a brand-new coat.

Chapter XII

MAXIMS FROM LORD CHESTERFIELD

The pages of the "Noble Oracle" are replete with sound advice, which all may receive with profit. Genuine politeness is the same always and everywhere.

—Madame Bienséance

CHEERFULNESS & GOOD HUMOR

It is a wonderful thing that so many persons, putting in claims to good breeding, should think of carrying their spleen into company, and entertaining those with whom they converse with a history of their pains, headaches, and [illnesses]. This is, of all others, the meanest help to social happiness; and a man must have a very mean opinion of himself, who, on having detailed his grievances, is accosted by asking the news.

Mutual good humor is a dress in which we ought to appear, whenever we meet; and we ought to make no mention of ourselves, unless it be in matters wherein our friends ought to rejoice. There is no real life but cheerful life; therefore [hypochondriacs] should be sworn before they enter into company not to say a word of themselves until the meeting breaks up.

THE ART OF PLEASING

The art of pleasing is a very necessary one to possess, but a very difficult one to acquire. It can hardly be reduced to rules; and your own good sense and observation will teach you more of it than I can.

- Do as you would be done by, is the surest method that I know of pleasing.
- Observe carefully what pleases you in others, and probably the same things in you will please others.
- If you are pleased with the complaisance and attention of others to you, depend upon it [that] the same complaisance and attention, on your part, will equally please them.
- Take the tone of the company you are in, and do not pretend to give it; be serious or gay, as you find the present humor of the company. This is an attention due from every individual to the majority.

ADAPTATION OF MANNERS

Ceremony resembles that base coin which circulates through a country by the royal mandate. It serves every purpose of real money at home, but is entirely useless if carried abroad. A person who should attempt to circulate his native trash in another country would be thought either ridiculous or culpable. He is truly well bred who knows when to value and when to despise those national peculiarities that are regarded by some with so much observance. A traveler of taste at once perceives that the wise are polite all the world over, but that fools are polite only at home.

BAD HABITS

Keep yourself free from strange tricks or habits, such as thrusting on your tongue, continually snapping your fingers, rubbing your hands, sighing aloud, gaping with a noise like a country fellow that has been sleeping in a hayloft, or indeed with any noise; and many others that I have noticed before. These are imitations of the manners of the mob, and are degrading to a gentleman. It is rude and vulgar to lean your head back and destroy the appearance of fine papered walls.

> Keep yourself free from strange tricks or habits.

DO WHAT YOU ARE ABOUT

Hoc age was a maxim among the Romans, which means, "Do what you are about, and do that only." A little mind is hurried by twenty things at once; but a man of sense does but one thing at a time, and resolves to excel in it; for whatever is worth doing at all, is worth doing well. Therefore, remember to give yourself up entirely to the thing you are doing, be it what it may, whether your book or your play; for if you have a right ambition, you will desire to excel all boys of your age, at cricket, at trap-ball, as well as in learning.

> A man of sense does but one thing at a time, and resolves to excel in it; for whatever is worth doing at all, is worth doing well.

PEOPLE WHO NEVER LEARN

There have been people who have frequented [fine events] all their lifetime, and yet have never divested themselves of their natural stiffness and awkwardness; but have continued as vulgar as if they were never out of a servants' hall. This has been owing to carelessness, and a want of attention to the manners and behavior of others.

CONFORMITY TO LOCAL MANNERS

Civility, which is a disposition to accommodate and oblige others, is essentially the same in every country; but good-breeding, as it is called, which is the manner of exerting that disposition, is different in almost every country, and merely local; and every man of sense imitates and conforms to that local good-breeding or the place which he is at.

HOW TO CONFER FAVORS

The greatest favors may be done so awkwardly and bunglingly as to offend; and disagreeable things may be done so agreeably as almost to oblige. Endeavor to acquire this great secret. It exists, it is to be found, and is worth a great deal more than the grand secret of the alchemists would be, if it were—as it is not—to be found.

FITNESS

One of the most important points of life is decency, which means doing what is proper, and where it is proper; for many things are proper at one time, and in one place, that are extremely improper in another. Read men, therefore, yourself, not in books, but in nature. Adopt no systems, but study them yourself.

HOW TO REFUSE

A polite manner of refusing to comply with the solicitations of a company is also very necessary to be learned; for a young man who seems to have no will of his own, but does everything that is asked of him, may be a very good-natured, but he is a very silly, fellow.

CIVILITY TO WOMEN

Civility is particularly due to all women; and remember that no provocation whatsoever can justify any man in not being civil to every woman; and the greatest man in the world would be justly reckoned a brute if he were not civil to the meanest woman.

SPIRIT

Spirit is now a very fashionable word. To act with spirit, to speak with spirit, means only to act rashly, and to talk indiscreetly. An able man shows his spirit by gentle words and resolute actions; he is neither hot nor timid.

Chapter XIII

ILLUSTRATIVE ANECDOTES

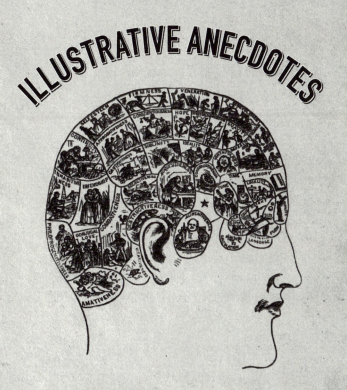

*It is well to combine amusement
with instruction, whether you write for young or old.*

—Anonymous

EXAMPLE #1: ELDER BLUNT & SISTER SCRUB

The house of the excellent Squire Scrub was the [traveler's] home; and a right sweet, pleasant home it would have been but for a certain unfortunate weakness of [in] the every other way *excellent* Sister Scrub. The weakness I allude to was, or at least it was suspected to be, *the love of praise*. Now, the good sister was really worthy of high praise, and she often received it; but she had a way of disparaging herself and her performances which some people thought was intended to invite praise.

No housewife kept her floors looking so clean and her walls so well whitewashed as she. Every board was scrubbed and scoured till further scrubbing and scouring would have been labor wasted. No one could look on her white ash floor and not admire the polish her industry gave it. The "Squire" was a good provider, and Sister Scrub was an excellent cook; and so their table groaned under a burden of good things on all occasions when good cheer was demanded.

And yet, you could never enter the house and sit half an hour without being reminded that "Husband held Court yesterday, and she couldn't keep the house decent." If you sat down to eat with them, she was sorry she "hadn't anything fit to eat." She had been scrubbing, or washing, or ironing, or she had been half sick, and she hadn't got such and such things that she ought to have. Nor did it matter how bountiful or how well prepared the repast really was, there was always *something* deficient, the want of which furnished a text for a disparaging discourse on the occasion.

I remember once that we sat down to a table that a king might have been happy to enjoy. There was the light snow-white bread; there were the potatoes reeking in butter; there were chickens swimming in gravy; there were the onions and the turnips, and I was sure Sister Scrub had gratified her ambition for once. We sat down, and a blessing was asked; instantly the good sister began; she was afraid her coffee was too much burned, or that the water had been smoked, or that she hadn't roasted the chicken enough. There ought to have been some salad, and it was too bad that there was nothing nice to offer us.

We, of course, endured those unjustifiable apologies as well as we could, simply remarking that everything was really nice, and proving by our acts that the repast was tempting to our appetites.

I will now introduce another actor to the reader—Elder Blunt, the circuit preacher. Elder Blunt was a good man. His religion was of the most genuine, experimental kind. He was a *very* plain man. He . . . would no more dare to preach a *fine* sermon than wear a fine coat. He was celebrated for his commonsense way of exhibiting the principles of religion. He *would* speak just what he thought, and as he felt. He somehow got the name of being an eccentric preacher, as every man, I believe, does who *never* prevaricates, and always acts and speaks as he thinks.

Somehow or other, Elder Blunt had heard of Sister Scrub, and that infirmity of hers, and he resolved to cure her. On his first round he stopped at "Squire Scrub's," as all other travelers had done before him. . . . The preacher entered the house [and] was shown into the best room, and soon felt very much at home. He expected to hear something in due time disparaging the domestic arrangements, but he heard it sooner than he expected.

This time, if Sister Scrub could be credited, her house *was* all upside down; it wasn't fit to stay in, and she was sadly mortified to be caught in such a plight. The elder looked all around the room, as if to observe the terrible disorder, but he said not a word.

By-and-by the dinner was ready, and the elder sat down with the family to a well-spread table. Here, again, Sister Scrub found everything faulty; the coffee wasn't fit to drink, and she hadn't anything fit to eat. The elder lifted his dark eye to her face; for a moment he seemed to penetrate her very soul with his austere gaze; then slowly rising from the table, he said, "Brother Scrub, I want my horse immediately; I must leave!"

"Why, Brother Blunt, what is the matter?"

"Matter? Why, sir, your house isn't fit to stay in, and you haven't anything fit to eat or drink, and I won't stay."

Both the "Squire" and his lady were confounded. This was a piece of eccentricity entirely unlooked for. They were stupefied. But the elder was gone. He wouldn't stay in a house not fit to stay in, and where there wasn't anything fit to eat and drink.

Poor Sister Scrub! She wept like a child at her folly. She "knew it would be all over town," she said, "and everybody would be laughing at her." And then, how should she meet the blunt, honest elder again? "She hadn't meant anything by what she had said." Ah! She never thought how wicked it was to say *so much* that didn't mean anything.

The upshot of the whole matter was, that Sister Scrub "saw herself as others saw her." She ceased making apologies, and became a wiser and better Christian. Elder Blunt always puts up there, always finds everything as it should be, and, with all his eccentricities, is thought by the family the most agreeable, as he is acknowledged by everybody to be the most consistent of men.

—*Rev. J. V. Watson*

EXAMPLE #2: JOHN & HIS HAT

Mr. Johnson, an English traveler, relates, in his notes on North America, the following story:

"At Boston," he says, "I was told of a gentleman in the neighborhood who, having a farm servant, found him very satisfactory in every respect, except that he invariably came into his employer's room with his hat on.

"'John,' said he to the man one day, 'you always keep your hat on when you come into the room.'

"'Well, sir,' said John, 'and haven't I a right to?'

"'Yes,' was his employer's reply, 'I suppose you have.'

"'Well,' said John, 'if I have a right to, why shouldn't I?'

"This was a poser from one man to another, where all have equal rights. So, after a moment's reflection the gentleman asked:

"'Now, John, what will you take, how much more wages will you ask, to take off your hat whenever you come in?'

"'Well, that requires consideration, I guess,' said the man.

"'Take the thing into consideration, then,' rejoined the employer, 'and let me know tomorrow morning.'

"The morrow comes, and John appears.

"'Well, John, have you considered what additional wages you are to have for taking your hat off?'

"'Well, sir, I guess it's worth a dollar a month.'

"'It's settled, then, John; you shall have another dollar a month.'

"So the gentleman retained a good man, while John's hat was always in his hand when he entered the house." . . .

But John is waiting, hat in hand, to hear what we have to say respecting his case.

We say that John was wrong in not taking off his hat voluntarily, but that the feeling that prevented his doing so was right. He was right in feeling that the accidental circumstance of his being a hired man gave his employer no claim to any special mark of respect from him; and, as he considered that the removal of his hat would have been a special mark of respect, and thus an acknowledgment of social inferiority, he declined to make that acknowledgment.

But John was mistaken. The act referred to would not have borne such an interpretation. John ought to have felt that on coming into the presence of a man, a fellow-citizen and co-sovereign, and particularly on entering his abode, one of the innumerable royal residences of the country, some visible sign of respect, some kind of deferential salutation, is *due* from the person entering.

John should have risen superior to the mere accident of his position, and remembered only that he and his employer were men and equals. The positions of the two men might be reversed in a day; their equality as men and citizens nothing but crime could affect.

—*James Parton*

EXAMPLE #3: A LEARNED MAN AT TABLE

Some of the many errors that are liable to be committed through ignorance of usage are pleasantly pointed out in the following story, which is related by a French writer:

The Abbé Cosson, professor in the *Collége Mazarin*, thoroughly accomplished in the art of teaching, saturated with Greek, Latin, and literature, considered himself a perfect well of science: he had no conception that a man who knew all Persius and Horace by heart could possibly commit an error—above all, an error at table. But it was not long before he discovered his mistake.

One day, after dining with the Abbé de Radonvilliers at Versailles, in company with several courtiers and marshals of France; he was boasting of the rare acquaintance with etiquette and custom that he had exhibited at dinner. The Abbé Delille, who heard this eulogy upon his own conduct, interrupted his harangue by offering to wager that he had committed at least a hundred improprieties at the table. "How is it possible?" exclaimed Cosson. "I did exactly like the rest of the company."

"What absurdity!" said the other. "You did a thousand things that no one else did. First, when you sat down at the table, what did you do with your napkin?"

"My napkin! Why, just what everybody else did with theirs. I unfolded it entirely, and fastened it to my buttonhole."

"Well, my dear friend," said Delille, "you were the only one that did *that*, at all events. No one hangs up his napkin in that style; they are contented with placing it on their knees. And what did you do when you took soup?"

"Like the others, I believe. I took any spoon in one hand and my fork in the other—"

"Your fork! Who ever ate soup with a fork? But to proceed: After your soup, what did you eat?"

"A fresh egg."

"And what did you do with the shell?"

"Handed it to the servant who stood behind my chair."

"Without breaking it, of course?"

"Well, my dear Abbé, nobody ever eats an egg without breaking the shell."

"And after your egg—?"

"I asked the Abbé Radonvilliers to send me a piece of the hen near him."

"Bless my soul! A piece of the *hen*! You never speak of hens excepting in the barnyard. You should have asked for fowl, or chicken. But you say nothing of your mode of drinking."

"Like all the rest, I asked for *claret* and *champagne*."

"Let me inform you, then, that persons always ask for *claret wine* and *champagne wine*. But tell me, how did you eat your bread?"

"Surely I did that properly. I cut it with my knife in the most regular manner possible."

"Bread should always be broken, not cut. But the coffee, how did you manage it?"

"It was rather too hot, and I poured a little of it into my saucer."

"Well, you committed here the greatest fault of all. You should never pour your coffee into the saucer, but always drink it from the cup."

The poor Abbé was confounded. He felt that though one might be master of the seven sciences, yet that there was another species of knowledge that, if less dignified, was equally important.

This occurred many years ago, but there is not one of the observances neglected by the Abbé Cosson which is not enforced with equal rigidness in the present day.

EXAMPLE #4: ENGLISH WOMEN IN HIGH LIFE

Lord Hardwicke's family consists of his countess, his eldest son (about eighteen or twenty, Lord Royston by courtesy), three of the finest-looking daughters you ever saw, and several younger sons. The daughters—Lady Elizabeth, Lady Mary, and Lady Agnita—are surpassingly beautiful; such development—such rosy cheeks, laughing eyes, and unaffected manners—you rarely see combined.

They take a great deal of outdoor exercise, and came aboard the *Merrimac*, in a heavy rain, with Irish shoes thicker soled than you or I ever wore, and cloaks and dresses almost impervious to wet. They steer their father's yacht, walk the Lord knows how many miles, and don't care a cent about rain, besides doing a host of other things that would shock our ladies to death; and yet in the parlor are the most elegant-looking women, in their satin shoes and diamonds, I ever saw. . . .

After dinner the ladies play and sing for us, and the other night they got up a game of blind-man's-buff [a variant of tag], in which the ladies said we had the advantage, inasmuch as their "petticoats rustled so that they were easily caught." They call things by their names here. In the course of the game, Lord Hardwicke himself was blindfolded, and, trying to catch someone, fell over his daughter's lap on the floor, when two or three of the girls caught him by the legs and dragged his lord-ship—roaring with laughter, as we all were—on his back into the middle of the floor.

Yet they are perfectly respectful, but appear on a perfect equality with each other.

—*Letter from an Officer of the* Merrimac

INDEX

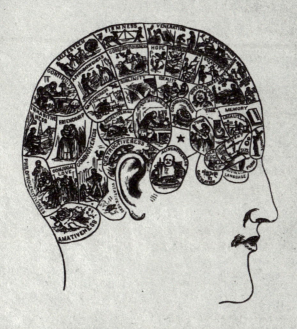